Sexual Identity

Sexual Identity

Ronald A. LaTorre

Nelson-Hall nh Chicago

Library of Congress cataloging in Publication Data

LaTorre, Ronald A
  Sexual identity.

  Bibliography: p.
  Includes index.
  1. Sex (Psychology)   2. Identity (Psychology)
3. Personality, Disorders of.   4. Mental health.
I.   Title.
BF692.2.L37   155.3'2   78-26442
ISBN 0-88229-360-5

Manufactured in the United States of America

10   9   8   7   6   5   4   3   2   1

". . . there is this dichotomy, that all the world has only two bathrooms: gentlemen and ladies." Carlfred Broderick, *Sexuality and Aging: An Overview*.

"It is evident that men and women play different roles. It can even be said that their concept of pleasure is different. In coitus, man is the Aggressive force, woman the Receptive, which is basically the role of the male and the female in nature itself. This difference in action is directly linked to a difference in concept. The man says of the act of love: 'This woman is united to me'; while the woman thinks: 'I am united to this man.'" Vatsyayana, *Kama Sutra: The Hindu Ritual of Love*.

Contents

Preface

An ever increasing amount of research has linked mental illness with a problem in sexual identification. Sexual identity is the core around which self-identity and personality are formed. An impairment in the establishment of a sexual identity results in a faulty personality structure. Even though researchers in this area and some mental health professionals have recognized this fact, information has been slowly and incompletely disseminated to the general public and to other professionals not directly involved with sexual identity problems. It is necessary that individuals learn the importance of sexual identity and the consequences of a faulty sexual identification. It is particularly critical that parents learn about this problem since their behavior toward the child basically helps to form the child's sexual identity. It is also important that mental health professionals recognize this area as a potential trouble source and deal with it more effectively than they have in the past.

This is not meant to be a handbook on how to raise a child, nor is it meant to be an exhaustive treatise on sexual identity. It is meant to serve both professionals and lay people as an introduction to the fascinating area of sexual identity, and, in fact, it is the first book on sexual identity and mental health written with the lay person in mind. The book should therefore be of interest to many types of individuals and of particular benefit to parents. Professionals not familiar with the subject may also find this book of great help and can use it to brush up their knowledge in an area of ever increasing importance. This book also offers the reader the opportunity to use a nonstandardized psychological test to measure his or her own masculinity-femininity.

I should like to thank a little-recognized individual—the research assistant. This is the person who usually does the bulk of the work for any research study but receives scant acknowledgment. The work is sometimes done for monetary reward, sometimes for course credit, and sometimes voluntarily. Without the research assistant, I could not have amassed sufficient research evidence to write this book. Therefore, I thank all those individuals who, at one time or another, served as my research assistants: Mary Ann Back, Amy Louise Borgeson, Nicole Edwards, Maxine Endman, Ilona Gossmann, Sharon Horlick, Karen Kear, Anne-Marie LaTorre, Judy LeGallais, Ellen Morrissy, Cynthia Patterson, Jane Perry, Cathy Roozman, Susan Seltzer, Allan Shapiro, and Kai Wing Tsang.

And a final thank you to my editor, Carol Rausch Gorski, for an excellent job.

I.
Sexual Identity

Once upon a time in a faraway land, there lived a king and queen who were very unhappy. They were unhappy because an evil witch had cast a spell on them so that they would have no children. This also meant that there would be no royal descendants from their line.

One day while the king was dragon hunting, he happened to chance upon a tiny dragon. "You are so small," the king said, "that I shall spare your life." The dragon, although tiny, was a magical dragon. "O great king, because you have spared my life, I shall give you two lives in return." The king did not know exactly what the dragon meant. However, when he returned to the castle that night he discovered the meaning of the dragon's words. He was greeted by an overly joyous queen who exclaimed, "I am with child! In fact, I am with children!" The queen was pregnant, and the court physician had determined that she would give birth to twins.

And so it was on the day of birth that two identical male children were born to the king and queen. They were so alike that there was absolutely no way to tell them apart. The king was very proud of his two sons and had great expectations for both of them. However, the evil witch who had originally cast the spell on the royal family was very angry that her spell had been broken by the magical dragon. She swore that she would avenge herself on the twin princes.

When the twins were seven months of age, the king and queen decided that they should be circumcised. The royal physician was summoned. But, since it was prohibited to spill royal blood, the physician was not allowed to use his surgical knife; so he sought the aid of the court magician. The magician had the power to harness the lightning bolts in the heavens. The physician guided the magician as together they used lightning bolts to circumcise the twins. The physician and magician succeeded in circumcising the first twin. During the circumcision of the second twin, however, the evil witch saw an opportunity to even the score with the royal family. Using her own black powers, she unleashed the heavens' energy, and lightning struck the child's penis with tenfold the force it should have, burning not only the foreskin but the entire penis right up to the abdomen. A royal penis was destroyed, and so was the king's pride.

For many months, the king and queen mourned for their son. The boy, being so young, was still oblivious to the social consequences although the mishap may have smarted somewhat. Finally, the kingdom's mentor offered sage advice. As a son, the twin would always be less than perfect; he would travel through life as a freak; he would always be aware of his deficiency; and he could incur great emotional anguish. But if the twin were a daughter, the child would be less imperfect in terms of outward signs.

The children were at this time seventeen months of

age. They were not yet fully aware of sexual distinctions but they were rapidly approaching that stage of awareness. A decision was promptly made. The king and queen were now to have a son and a daughter.

The queen ordered that the boy's (henceforth the "girl's") wardrobe be changed. All her pants were dyed pink, frilly blouses were sewn, and gowns of all colors were presented to the "princess." Jewelry fit only for a princess was obtained. The little girl received rings, necklaces, bracelets, and broaches. Ribbons now adorned her hair, which grew very long. She played with dolls and doll castles, toy brooms, and pots and pans. She was tutored in the utmost etiquette. She learned the social graces and joined her mother in the daily activities of the castle. The princess grew up disliking dirt and trying always to be neat and proper.

The prince's wardrobe consisted of pants and shirts, chain mail suits, and armor. He was taught the finer arts of swordsmanship, jousting, wrestling, dragon killing, and damsel saving. He was given gifts of swords and shields, ponies, toy knights, and baby dragons. He rough-and-tumbled with the other nobles' children and detested baths. He spent his days outside the castle with his father. Very much unlike his sister, he paid little attention to etiquette. He wiped his mouth on his shirt-sleeves and threw his chicken bones over his shoulder.

The prince grew up into a handsome lad, and the princess matured into a beautiful lady. And, except for their nobility, they were no different than any other man and woman. The prince did manly things, and the princess did womanly things. The princess liked to sew clothes, while the prince preferred to sow wild oats.

And so it was—or so the story goes—that in this faraway land a normal biological male (one of an identical twin pair) was transformed into a female. Only, the land is not so far away and the event not so rare. It happened in the United States—not to kings and not by magic, but to normal individuals by normal medical professionals. The incident is described in detail in *Man & Woman, Boy & Girl* (Money and Ehrhardt 1972), and an abbreviated account is given here.

A man and a woman brought their identical male twins to be circumcised by electrocautery. An error was made, the electrical current was too powerful, and one child's penis was burned completely to the abdomen. The parents sought advice for many months. One suggestion was to reassign the sex of the child and make him a female (a not uncommon event for children born with ambiguous or malformed genitals).

The parents decided to reassign the sex of the injured child and immediately started to treat the two children differently, in line with society's sex role standards. The first apparent change was in clothes and hairdo. The mother first purchased pink pants and frilly blouses for the reassigned twin, and she later bought her daughter dresses. Nightwear for the female twin became granny gowns. The female twin, unlike her brother, was encouraged to wear bracelets and hair ribbons. Her hair was left to grow long. As she was growing up, she showed a decided preference for dresses, and she took pride in her long hair.

Etiquette and neatness were other areas in which the twins differed. Encouraged, again, by the parents' differential treatment of the two children, the little girl disliked being dirty. She would be upset if she were messy or her clothes were soiled. The little boy, on the other hand, disliked being cleaned. Like other little boys, he would make a fuss when his mother tried to wash him.

At Christmas, the girl wanted and received dolls, a doll carriage, and a doll house. The little boy received a garage with cars, pumps, and tools. As is obvious, the toy preferences were in line with appropriate future gender roles. The dolls and doll-related toys allowed rehearsal of the maternal aspects of the female adult role, and the car-related toys allowed the boy to rehearse one possible future male role. In fact, the little girl mimicked many of the mother's domestic roles. For example, she tidied up the house and cleaned the kitchen. The boy, on the other hand, preferred to rough-and-tumble outside. He further expressed a desire to be like daddy and to one day go to work carrying a lunch kit.

One day the little boy pulled down his pants in the front yard and urinated. He was quite proud of himself, and the mother, in response, laughed about it (a not-too-subtle encouragement). However, a totally different reaction occured when one day the little girl took off her panties and threw them over a fence. The mother spanked the little girl—not because she threw her panties over the fence but because she no longer had any panties on herself. The mother told the little girl that "nice little girls" don't do things like that and that from then on she should keep her panties on.

At the last written report the children were about eight years old. To any unknowing observer, they are normal male and female children. And in actions, dress, mannerisms, perferences, and even thinking, they are male and female—not two males. Anatomically, the female child is really a male who is lacking a penis. But with the aid of hormones and the creation of an artificial vagina when the body is mature, the children will even look like an anatomical male and female, respectively.

I think the history of these twins is one of the best accounts of the ways in which parents instill different sex roles in children. The emphasis should be placed on the fact, that, although these children were originally identical twin boys, the parents by their differential attitudes and behavior towards the youngsters were able to raise one of them in line with society's standards for the male and the other in accord with society's standards for the female. The story illustrates a fundamental point. Male and female anatomy exists at birth, but maleness and femaleness develop as the child develops. As is evident from the story, the development of maleness and femaleness is largely dependent on the parents' training the child in one or the other alternative. Others' interactions with the child also help to socialize it into either a male or a female role.

Also, it should be apparent that maleness and femaleness need not necessarily be congruent with the child's biological sex. That is to say, the anatomical sex of the child does not automatically lead to the proper psychological sex. A biological male, even one with a normal penis, could develop many female qualities, even to the extent that he is more female than he is male. In fact, some biological males and females feel so estranged from their biological sex that, as adults, they seek and obtain anatomical sex changes by surgical means.

It is precisely the facts that psychological sex must develop, that it is not necessarily congruent with the biological sex of the individual, and that psychological difficulties can arise from a problem in the development of psychological sex that make this an area of importance and interest to psychological specialists.

Men and women have always been aware that, besides anatomical differences, there exist psychological differences between the two sexes. However, it has only been within the last century that the subject has gained scientific prominence. Even so, it probably still has not attained the recognition it deserves.

Many would shrug off "sexual identity" or "psychological sex" in terms such as "Raquel Welch is a real woman—she has such a great pair" or "John Wayne is a he-man 'cause he don't take no shit from nobody." But sexual identity consists of much more than physical attributes or a few aspects of personality. In fact, a clear delineation of the meaning of sexual identity has been lacking, and this lack has been a major factor in the confusion that presently exists in this area of psychology. One can hardly examine something when he is unsure precisely what it is. Prior to further discussion of sexual identity, then, it is necessary to define the term as used in this book.

I shall offer now what I believe to be the most concise and complete set of conceptions. For those with advanced interest in this area, a comparison of my definitions with those of other researchers is given in Table I. For the average reader, suffice it to say that almost every individual who discusses sexual identity sets up his or her own definitions and personal terminology. As a result, there can be little comparison among these people's thoughts, ideas, and research findings. The definitions I offer are developed from those of others.

Sexual identity, in its broadest sense, has been compared to a symphony. A symphonic orchestration has many motifs that are worked into one integrated theme, and the same is true of sexual identity. However, with sexual identity it can happen that the motifs are discordant and the theme is considerably less than integrated. The major motifs of sexual identity are worked around gender identity, gender role adoption, gender role preference, and gender role ability. I have used the word *gender* rather than the word *sex* because the latter has connotations of reproductive functioning that the former does not have— and reproduction is but a part of the overall picture. However, since popular usage lends familiarity to the word *sex* I have allowed myself to retain it to indicate the overall theme that I call sexual identity.

GENDER IDENTITY

Gender identity is used to mean a self-definition as being male or female. It is regarded as a very deep belief that may even be unconscious. This means that, while most people can say "I am a male" or "I am a female," what they say may not be what they actually feel or believe. The point of determining one's gender identity will be dealt with later. Gender identity is the first level of sexual identity that is developed. In a sense, it is a core

Table 1
Comparisons of definitions used in this book with the
definitions used by other reseachers

Definitions of sexual identity used in this book

Definitions used by	Gender Identity	Gender Role Adoption	Gender Role Preference	Gender Role Ability
J. Money				
gender identity	XX			
gender role		XX		
H. Biller				
sex role identity/ orientation	XX			
sex role adoption		XX		
sex role preference			XX	
R. Green				
basic conviction of being male/female	XX			
behaviors culturally associated with being male/female		XX		
preference for male/female sex partners			X	
D. McClelland & N. Watt				
gender identity	XX			
sex role style		X		
gender typed interests, likes, and attitudes		XXX	XXX	

"X" indicates that the other author's definition includes only a part of the definition used in this book.

"XX" indicates that the other author's definition is directly comparable to the definition used in this book.

"XXX" indicates that the other author's definition is more comprehensive than the definition used in this book.

around which a definition of the self and, later, personality will be formed.

Gender identity is relatively resistant to change once it has been firmly established. The concept of male/female is linked with the use of language, and it is no coincidence that gender identity establishes itself as language develops. Hence, gender identity is in the process of formation around the age of eighteen months. Experience with sex reassignment supports the theory that gender identity is formed at about this age. If a child is reassigned prior to eighteen months of age, it will develop a gender identity congruent with its reassigned sex. However, the greater the duration between eighteen months of age and the age of sex reassignment, the more problematic is the sex reassignment for the child involved. An older child has developed or partially developed his gender identity and has to adopt an entirely different self-concept and self-definition.

Theoretically, the establishment of a gender identity is intimately linked with the development of a body image. Body image is the way one views his own body and his satisfaction with that view. Body image helps to develop gender identity in two ways. First, a child learns what a male body is and what a female body is—naked or with certain clues such as clothing and hairstyle. This information is compared to the child's own body. By this process, children self-categorize their bodies and themselves. Second, others see the child's body with its external clues, and these others give various forms of feedback to the child. For example, on a bus recently I heard a woman say to a little girl who was a stranger to her, "Pull your dress down, honey. Ladies don't sit like that. And remember, you are a lady." The visual clues of a dress and long hair signalled the woman to speak to the child in such a way that the girl, in no uncertain terms, was given feedback as to her body image. In fact, even the assignment of sex at birth ("Congratulations! You have a boy/girl.") is dependent on the doctor's perception of the body image. This initial sex assignment is probably the most important feedback the child will ever receive concerning its body image, as we shall see in Chapter 2.

Gender Role Adoption

At about the time that he is developing his gender identity, the child notices certain roles are expected of males and certain roles are expected of females. He also notices that certain roles are discouraged for males and certain roles are discouraged for females. Such characteristics as traits, behavior, and appearance that differentiate the sexes are known as gender roles. Almost all of these gender roles are common knowledge, and it would be beyond the scope of this book to discuss them all here.

The child is learning gender roles as he is learning which role or roles he is to adopt himself. Gender role adoption refers to those aspects of gender role that the individual actually acquires. The adopted characteristics may be conscious or unconscious to the individual but should be readily observable to others. For example, a female may be seen as masculine by her friends but may herself actually feel that she is very feminine. This discrepancy could arise in one of several ways. It is possible that the female is outrightly deceiving herself; it is possible that the female and the observers have different definitions of femininity (as would occur with a female being observed by members of another culture); or, more probably, there is a differential emphasis on the many aspects of the female role. That is, the female may notice that she wears makeup, has a feminine hairdo, wears dresses, and makes love only with males. She labels herself feminine. Others, however, may note that she walks like a lumberjack, sits with her legs spread open, and uses extremely profane language. They might label her as masculine. As another example, consider how many males have been labeled as effeminate merely because they talk with a sibilant *S* or have a limp wrist, despite all the masculine characteristics they possess.

It should be clear from the preceding paragraphs that I believe a person learns masculine and feminine traits from the environment, and especially from the parents. This point will be discussed in greater detail in Chapter 2. However, I should specify at this point that the content of the two roles is culturally determined. A good deal of anthropological evidence proves that what is considered masculine in one culture is considered feminine in another. And, because the content is culturally determined, it is not only possible that content may be different across cultures, but also different within a culture over a period of time. In fact we are currently being faced in the United States and Canada with minor shifts in gender role. Actually, the state of affairs is more of a merger toward gender-role neutrality than it is toward gender-role reversal. In a recent study, William Piper and I (LaTorre and Piper 1978) found that a sexual identity test developed in the 1930s still differentiated males and females in the 1970s. Gender role reversals on this test were rare, but a number of gender-differentiating items had become gender neutral, or unrelated to an individual's gender.

Gender Role Preference

Another aspect of sexual identity is gender role preference. This is an individual's preference for sex-typed items or behavior. It differs from adoption of gender role in that it addresses itself to what a person would like to adopt and not what he has actually adopted. For the most part, one's preference coincides with one's adoption. A man who prefers to have sex with females probably will. But in some instances adoption and preference do not coincide. For example, a man might prefer to be a famous boxer (a very masculine profession) but finds himself, instead, an accountant.

Gender Role Ability

A final aspect of the overall theme of sexual identity is gender role ability—a person's ability to present manifest acquired skills and behaviors that are defined as aspects of the gender role. As an example, let us assume that part of the male role is to be assertive. Two males may both be assertive, but one more so than the other. The former has greater ability in the gender role of assertiveness.

Relationships of Identity and Roles

Typically, a person's gender identity and the three aspects of his or her gender role (adoption, preference, and ability) are congruent with regard to whether they are basically male or basically female. However, they may at times or in specific individuals be discrepant with one another.

In research work with nonpatient homosexuals, it has been determined that homosexuals are basically secure and confident members of their biological sex. That is to say, their gender identity is congruent with their biological sex. However, there is considerable variation in their adoption of gender roles. Some homosexual males, for example, do try to mimic females in dress, mannerisms, or both, while other homosexual males adopt a male gender role. This illustrates that gender identity and gender role adoption are independent aspects within the overall sexual identity theme.

Prisoners serve as a good example of how gender role preference may be discrepant with gender role adoption. Due to the lack of females, many prisoners have been known to have sexual relations in prison with other male prisoners. Yet these same persons may voice a preference for a female and if allowed to choose would have sex with a female rather than another male. So gender role adoption (sex with another male) is not congruent with gender role preference (sex with a female) for this select group.

The independence of gender role ability is demonstrated by transsexual males (biological males who seek sex change surgery as adults to become females). These males have a female gender identity, a female gender role adoption, and a female gender role preference. But they differ considerably in their ability to "pass" as female. Some adapt well and present themselves as normal females; others maintain a masculine gait and mannerisms.

Sexual identity is thus composed of gender identity and gender roles which in the average individual are congruent. However, these motifs are independent and can therefore be discordant.

In addition, while sexual identity is dichotomous (male/female), gender roles are multidimensional, and so we may find congruence or incongruence within each of the three categories of gender role. For example, with reference to gender role adoption we could speak of adoption of sex-typed knowledge, behavior, appearance, and mannerisms. These various aspects are independent of one another. One could act effeminate (e.g. limp wrist), yet have the same knowledge that is typical for males to possess (e.g. how many players on a baseball team).

Any one of the major areas of gender role adoption can be further broken down. The area of appearance might be subdivided into dress, poise, gait, and posture. And within the area of gait one could determine whether an individual walks with small, mincing steps, if the thighs rub together when he walks, if there is a bounce or skip to the walk, and if the buttocks noticeably roll up and down.

Even though gender role encompasses an extremely large and often unrelated set of qualities, each specific quality is itself either unidimensional or dichotomous. For example, either an individual rolls his buttocks noticeably or he does not. Naturally, there are gradations and there are cases in which it will be difficult to definitively label a specific individual.

Obviously, since the specifics are independent, an individual may have some traits regarded as masculine and others regarded as feminine. For example, a male might constantly stroke his mustache, and some people regard stroking as a feminine trait. On the other hand he has demonstrated his masculinity by growing a mustache. This fact has led some individuals to suggest that masculinity and femininity are independent and are totally unrelated. I think this view is an overstatement. Masculinity and femininity may appear independent if independent specifics are examined and compared directly. For example, a female might suggest femininity by rolling her buttocks, but the same female might show masculinity by sitting with one calf crossed over the knee of her other leg. One might say, then, that in this female there exist both masculinity and femininity which are therefore independent. However, the independence of masculinity and femininity only appears to be true because of the direct comparison of a limited number of specifics.

I believe that each specific can be either masculine or feminine, not both. At any one point in time, on any one specific, one cannot display both masculinity and femininity—one either rolls the buttocks or one does not. Each independent specific, therefore, is unidimensional or dichotomous. It is true that one can possess various numbers of masculine or feminine specifics; however, any one specific ranges from masculine to feminine on just one scale.

Another concept related to sexual identity is that of androgyny. As used herein, androgyny means a condition in which an individual has about as many masculine as feminine specifics. The more the masculine specifics outnumber the feminine specifics, the more masculine is the person. The possession of mostly masculine specifics would be appropriate sex typing for a male and sex reversal for a female. Similarly, the more an individual's feminine specifics outnumber his or her masculine specifics, the more that person is said to be feminine. A preponderance of feminine traits is appropriate sex typing for a female and sex reversal for a male.

One final concept needs to be introduced. The original definition of androgyny included two types of people: (1) those who displayed a large number of masculine and feminine specifics of about equal number, and (2) those whose masculine or feminine characteristics were few but still about equal in number. That is to say, balance was the key to the original concept of androgyny. However, it has been argued that the two types of individuals within this category could be quite distinct (Spence, Helmreich, and Stapp 1975).

Therefore, the term *androgynous* is probably best reserved for those who display a large number of both male and female specifics. Those who display few male and female specifics will be referred to as undifferentiated. For example, one-year-old children display few sex-typed specifics. They are therefore undifferentiated. Undifferentiation can only exist because the range from masculine to feminine of each specific includes a point that is neither masculine nor feminine. The more of a person's specifics that are near this point, the more that person is undifferentiated. A graphic representation of androgyny, masculinity, femininity, and undifferentiation is shown in Figure 1.

SUMMARY

Sexual identity comprises several subcategories. At the first, or basic, level is a person's belief that he or she is male or female. This belief, which forms the core of sexual identity, is largely dependent on both the person's perception of his or her body image and on the messages received from significant others. This is the most important subcategory because it is mainly unconscious and can affect the development of subsequent levels. Another subcategory of sexual identity is gender role adoption, which consists of such acquired characteristics as traits, behavior, and appearance. The two remaining subcatego-

Figure 1
Graphic representation of the concepts androgyny,
masculinity, feminity, and undifferentiation

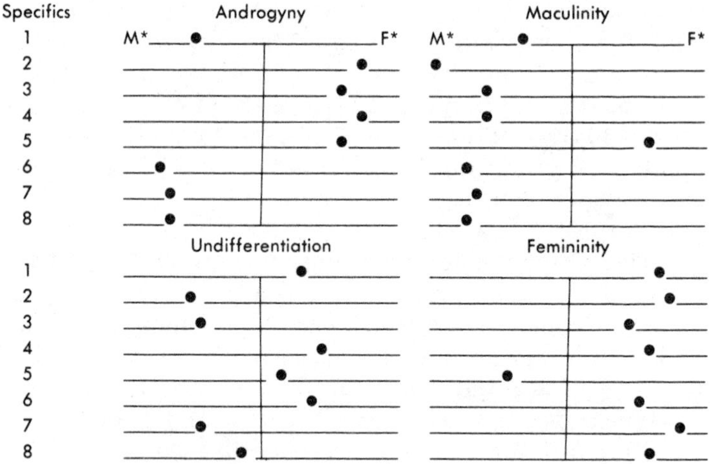

Note: M and F represent the masculine pole and the feminine pole, respectively.

ries are gender role preference and gender role ability. In most individuals, these four categories are congruent, but in some personalities a discrepancy exists at one or more levels. For example, even though most nonpatient male homosexuals describe themselves as male, they differ considerably in the degree to which they adopt the masculine or feminine role. Each of the three gender role subcategories is a multidimensional construct consisting of many specifics. A person can be masculine, feminine, or undifferentiated on any one specific, so that overall one can possess both masculine and feminine specifics. The more equally a person's specifics are distributed between masculine and feminine, the more that person is said to be androgynous—provided both kinds of traits are present in large number. An undifferentiated individual is one who displays little behavior that is distinctively masculine or feminine.

II.

The Development of Sexual Identity

Prior to the twentieth century, there was little study of how boys become men and girls become women. But parents' active attempts at differential training of the two sexes indicate that, even then, people thought sexual identity to be a learned, not inherited, phenomenon. In fact, about the only thing we can say with some certainty is that one is not born with a sexual identity. It develops in some way after birth.

A basic premise following from this is that each of us could have developed the sexual identity of either sex. In other words, at birth we were undifferentiated and had the potential to develop either a masculine or a feminine sexual identity. In fact, hormonal studies have demonstrated that each of us had the potential, while we were developing within our mother's womb, to develop *anatomically* into either a male or a female. While this book is concerned with psychological sex and not biological

17

sex, the latter aspect needs to be introduced to clarify an important point. That point is that, with regard to sexual identity, anatomy is not destiny.

Prenatal Sexual Development

Within the female's egg (ovum) and the male's sperm are chromosomes. These carry what may be considered the blueprints that are followed in the physical building of each individual. The typical chromosomal count is forty-six chromosomes. In the male, two of these chromosomes are labeled X and Y and are known as the sex chromosomes. The female's sex chromosomes are known as XX. From cases of chromosomal abnormalities (i.e. people born with one or more than two sex chromosomes) we are fairly certain that the presence of a single Y chromosome is the basis for the male blueprint. A single Y, regardless of the number of X chromosomes, normally produces a biological male (although a single Y without any X chromosomes is lethal). The absence of a Y chromosome allows the development of a biological female from a fertilized ovum with a single X or several X chromosomes.

The function of the Y chromosome appears to be that it specifies the development of the male gonads, the testes. In fact, the specification of the testes and the specification of hairy ears are the only known functions of the Y sex chromosome. The same embryonic structure that develops into the male testes would develop into the female ovaries in the absence of a Y chromosome.

If testes develop, they eventually secrete male hormones, which in turn act on other embryonic structures and cause them to differentiate into male internal accessory reproductive structures (e.g. the vas deferens and the prostate gland). In the absence of male hormones, the internal accessory reproductive structures differentiate into those typical for a female (e.g. the fallopian tubes and the uterus).

Shortly after the internal organs have begun to develop, the external genitals differentiate according to the same principle. If male hormone is present, a tiny embryonic structure enlarges and becomes the penis, and a fusion occurs in two folds of tissue to create the scrotum into which the testes will later descend. In the absence of male hormone, the same structure that would become the male's penis remains small and becomes the female's clitoris. Also, the two folds of tissue do not unite; instead, they become the outer vaginal lips.

Normally, this entire process occurs without a hitch after a gonad is determined on the basis of the sex chromosomes. However difficulties sometimes arise. For example, the testes may be deficient and secrete less male hormone than needed to stimulate the embryonic tissue. When this happens, the internal and external reproductive structures may become feminized, so that a genetic or chomosomal male has a feminine anatomy. On the other hand, an exogenous source of male hormone may be transmitted to a genetically female embryo. Male hormones are sometimes administered to women for medical reasons, and, if the woman is in early pregnancy, the male hormone may act on the embryonic tissue (whether genetically male or female) in much the same way that the hormone from the embryonic male's testes would act on the tissue. In this case, a genetic and gonadal female may become masculinized. In fact, if the male hormone is administered to a genetic female after differentiation of the internal organs, but prior to the differentiation of the external organs, the internal organs will be those typical for a female and the external organs will be masculinized.

In brief, then, the Y chromosome determines the specification of a set of testes that produce male hormones that cause embryonic structures to differentiate into male internal and external reproductive organs. The absence of a Y chromosome allows ovaries to differentiate, and the absence of male hormones allows the development of female internal and external reproductive organs.

However, errors and accidents do sometimes occur, so that one or more of these anatomical/hormonal sex differences may be discordant or incongruous with the rest. When such an event happens with reference to anatomy, the individual is known as a pseudohermaphrodite. He is called a *pseudo*hermaphrodite since he has only one set of sex organs, albeit they are incongruent. A true hermaphrodite has complete sets of sex organs of both sexes but no such case is known to have occurred in humans.

Sex Assignment

The entire differentiation process, whether normal or abnormal, results in an individual who shortly after birth is sex-assigned by the delivery doctor. This is the old "Congratulations, you have a boy/girl" routine. Normally, all the delivery doctor is concerned with is the morphology of the external genitalia. Therefore, in those cases in which differentiation was not normal, the assigned sex may be discrepant with one or all of the following: chromosomes, gonads, hormones, and internal accessory reproductive structures. In fact, in some cases the assigned sex is discrepant with the external genitalia. For example, some chromosomal females are born with a fusion of the vaginal labia and an enlarged clitoris which together give the appearance of a scrotum and tiny penis. Some of these individuals are sex-assigned as males and some as females.

In order to test the effects of various aspects of biological sex against the effects of assigned sex, a study was made of individuals whose assigned sex was discrepant with one or more biological determinants of sex (Hampson and Hampson 1961).

Thirty individuals were determined to have an assigned sex that was discrepant with their chromosomal sex. In all thirty cases, the individual's sexual identity was congruent with his assigned sex. Hence, chromosomes could be said to have had, in and of themselves, no effect on sexual identity.

Thirty individuals' gonadal sex was discrepant with their assigned sex. In all but three of these cases, the sexual identity was congruent with the assigned sex. Gonads, then, seem to have less influence on sexual identity than does sex assignment.

Thirty-one individuals were assigned to a sex that was discrepant with their sex hormones. All but five of these individuals displayed the sexual identity congruent with their assigned sex. Sex hormones, too, seem less powerful than assigned sex.

Twenty-five individuals were determined to have a sex assignment that contradicted the sex associated with their internal accessory reproductive organs. The sexual identity of all but three of these individuals was more congruent with their assigned sex than with their internal accessory organs.

Finally, there were twenty-five individuals whose external genital anatomy was discrepant with their assigned sex. In all but two of these cases, sexual identity was more congruent with assigned sex than with genital morphology. This seems quite amazing since, not only the doctor who sex-assigned, but also the parents and the child himself were surely aware that the child's genitals were not those typical of a person of his sex but were, in fact, more similar to a person's of the opposite sex. It should be noted, however, that this group displayed the most psychological distress. Obviously, the discrepancy was apparent enough to cause problems, but sexual identity developed along the lines of the sex that others thought the child was and not along the lines of what sex the child anatomically looked most like.

Until now I have been using sex of assignment in contrast with biological factors. This may have given the impression that there is something magical about a doctor, and if he says, "You are a boy," the person will become, psychologically, a boy. The magic is not in the doctor's incantations but in the process that is set into motion once the doctor has made his pronouncement.

This process, which leads to the development of a sexual identity, will be the topic for the remainder of this chapter.

The Development of Sexual Identity

The sense of being male or female is nurtured from birth onward. The sex of your child and his health are about the only two things your doctor tells you about him. In fact, besides a few other physical characteristics (length and weight) and a name you choose for the child (which is either a male or a female name), the child's sex and health are about the only thing *you* know about him even after seeing him and interacting with him.

From this moment on, you treat the child as though he were a member of his sex, which he is, and as though he possessed all the qualities of his sex, which he does not. Even in the same family, there are quantitative and qualitative differences in the parents' interactions with their children dependent on each child's sex.

Several studies have confirmed the mother's differential treatment of male and female children. This differential treatment could be the result of the mother's internalized expectations of males and females. It could also be the result of conscious or unconscious fostering of masculine or feminine traits, although much of the nurturing seems not to be a conscious effort to develop masculinity or femininity. In fact, mothers themselves not only do not realize their differential treatment but also deny that they do treat male and female infants differently.

Some of the differences noted have been that the limbs are exercised and stretched more for boy infants and that parents more often imitate the vocal babblings of girl infants. These are both in line with sexual identity expectations. The male is supposed to rely more on his musculature and the female is supposed to be more apt at verbal skills.

A little later in infancy, boys are allowed less physical contact and less verbal and eye contact than are infant girls. Male children are more likely than females to be held facing away from the parents rather than facing toward them. Also, the mother and father point out something in the environment more readily to a boy than to a girl infant. This would appear to be an attempt (probably unconscious) to develop independence, adventure, and mastery in the boy. In fact, by the age of thirteen months, there are clear differences between male and female children. The males show much more exploratory and autonomous behavior (Lewis 1972).

With regard to such differential treatment of infant children (who are actually undifferentiated), Kleeman (1971) has used the term "illusion." By this he means that parents treat the child according to what they wish him or her to become, not according to what the infant actually is. Illusion influences the ultimate result, so that the expectations that are set up usually are met. For example, when a mother dresses a three-month-old infant girl in a dress with a frilly bonnet, or when a father responds to an infant girl as if she were distinctly feminine, they are both acting on the basis of illusion.

This is not to say that illusion or differential behavior toward the sexes is wrong. In fact, illusion can be of great benefit in the parental conveyance of sexual identity to the child.

Even nursing of the infant is an area wherein differential treatment of the sexes occurs. Toward the infant male, the mother has a tendency to yield to his demands. When the little boy wants to suckle, the breast is there and ready. However, the female infant is given more direction. She more often has to yield to the mother's ideas of when and how much is best to eat. Again, this reflects sexual identity expectations: the male is eager, impatient, assertive, and dominant, while the female is yielding, interdependent, and reserved.

Between five and seven months of age, the infant begins to differentiate daddy and mommy by their voices, appearance, and touch. If you would like to test this, try to let the secondary caretaker (usually the father) cuddle the child when it is ill. This is the beginning of sex discrimination, which is necessary for sexual identity development.

Another important developmental milestone occurring around the seventh month is the "stranger reaction." Whereas previously the child sought only comfort, it now seeks comfort only from those it knows. Strangers make it anxious, and the infant may even cry when confronted by an unknown face.

The stranger reaction and the discrimination of mother and father lead to the infant's realization that he is himself a unique entity. He begins to differentiate himself from significant others, such as his mother. This lays the foundation for the subsequent formation of sexual identity and self-identity.

And, at about the same age of seven months, an interest in mirrors is noted. The child may often excitedly press various parts of his anatomy against the mirror. He examines his own mirror image. This activity helps give the child a mental representation of his body parts.

All this time, the child has been exploring his body. He plays with his fingers, mouth, feet, genitals, and other parts of his body, which provide feedback for the developing sense of self.

The self-concept serves as a frame of reference, a point of stability, the main organizing principle available in dealings with the social and physical worlds. The basic sense of self is developing all the time in the infant. It will eventually include, among other things, body image, feelings of the body, and sexual identification. In this sense, gender identity will become a cornerstone for all the subidentities that the individual will subsequently develop and that will interact with other subidentities to form the personality and the being of the individual.

The emerging gender identity is the result of many maturational factors, including increasing independence, mobility, and mental capacity and a clearer body image. It appears that the first conscious or unconscious experience of oneself as male or female, the image of oneself as male or female, the knowledge and confidence that one belongs to either the male or the female sex is crystalized around the age of eighteen months.

Eighteen months is set as the age of gender identity formation because, prior to this age, sex reassignment seems to have little adverse psychological effect on the child. The longer the duration between eighteen months of age and the age at which the sex of the individual is reassigned, the greater is the chance that the child will suffer psychological distress. To change a child's sex at a time much beyond the age of eighteen months can produce serious psychological harm.

Shortly before eighteen months, the child is able to differentiate pictures of boys and girls or men and women when asked to point to appropriate pictures. It must be soon after that when the child types himself according to sex, on the basis of his own body image.

The role of language in the development of sexual identity should not be underestimated. It is also around eighteen months that the child begins to speak. Body parts get specific names; the child has its own sex-typed name. Depending on the availability of pictures, parental or sibling nudity, and especially a discussion of anatomical differences, the child soon learns, in language related to body image, the distinctions between males and females and to which subset he belongs. It is no wonder, then, that gender identity crystalizes at about this age.

Gender Role Adoption

It becomes apparent to the child that gender distinctions are not meaningless. They actually entail a list of preferred 'do's' and 'don'ts'. Until now, the child has been a passive recipient of differential gender role training. Now he can begin to actively choose his role, even though people are still training him in it.

So around the age of two to three years, with the development of a sense of autonomy, the child has learned which sex he is and begins to learn what it means to be that sex. The child incorporates the beginnings of behavior and attitude patterns that will be positively valued by the self and others if they correspond to his assigned sex. He also learns to avoid behaviors and attitudes appropriate to the opposite sex, because they would be negatively valued should he adopt them.

It is largely the parents who influence the child's conception of positively and negatively valued behaviors and attitudes. However, significant others such as uncles, aunts, grandparents, and, much later, peers, teachers, and other authority figures also contribute to the child's construction of positive and negative values for different behaviors.

The knowledge of different role behavior for the two sexes is aided by the increased interaction between father and child as the child matures. The father, who largely remains in the background until the child starts to walk and talk, is now a major force in the child's life. The child can see clear differences between his mother and father. As time goes by, he observes other role models who are similar to the prototype models demonstrated by his parents.

By the age of four or five years, almost every child says that when he grows up he will be a parent of the appropriate sex (i.e. daddy if he is a boy and mommy if she is a girl). Also at this age, many or most of society's gender role standards are known. For example, the child can tell you fairly accurately which sex is associated with which occupations.

In fact, children as young as three years can make fairly accurate discriminations between male and female types of activities and possessions (Schell and Silber 1968). Three-year-olds were asked to look at a stick-figure drawing called "It." They were asked to think of It as a boy and as a girl. They were then asked to indicate preferences for It among various pictures of sex-typed objects, figures, and activities. Overall, the children did well on this sex-discrimination task; however, the girls discriminated better. Boys tended to choose more masculine activities for both the boy It and the girl It, even though discrimination was still demonstrated.

The fact that girls can make sex discriminations earlier than boys supports what has long been suggested in the literature. That is that boys have more difficulty developing sexual identity than girls do. Boys, like girls, begin with mother as the primary interactor. But for the boy, mother's behaviors become negatively valued as a role model, and he must adopt the father as the primary model. The girl continues with the mother as her model and adopts mother's behavior. In essence, a boy must leave mommy in order to adopt appropriate roles, but, for a girl, the adoption of such roles involves no transition between parents.

After learning to discriminate gender role behaviors and beginning to adopt appropriate ones, the child starts to rehearse them, or "try out his wings." The rehearsal of gender role is prevalent in play behavior. The boys are the soldiers, the cops, the robbers, the motorcyclists, the cavalry. There is a lot of action, mobility, and violence. The play involves real or imaginary items that increase mobility (bicycles and horses) or can do harm (knives, swords, and guns). The girls are mommies, nurses, and teachers. There is little action, but more interaction between playmates. The games take place within one vicinity. Items included tend to be more real (pots and pans, baby carriages, books) than imaginary.

The play behavior, which is encouraged by parents who buy the guns, balls, and doll houses, can actually be seen to reflect sex differences along what Parsons and Bales (1953) have termed the instrumental/expressive axis. Instrumentality is a concern for the relations between groups and the outside world. Expressiveness is a concern for harmonious relations among the members of a group. Parsons and Bales reported that, even in seventy-five primitive societies, biological sex served as the main axis for instrumental/expressive differentiation. Males in all societies tend to be instrumental while females are more often expressive.

More recently, Bakan (1966) used the terms agency and communion. Agency refers to the individual's manifestations of self-protection, self-assertion, and self-expansion. Communion is the individual's existence within a larger group and is manifested by a sense of being at one with others in that group.

Bakan's concept of agency and communion is similar to Parsons and Bales' instrumental/expressive distinction, if not identical. However, individuals involved with the feminist movement have decided to adopt Bakan's terms for the following reason. Parsons and Bales believed that a sex distinction between instrumentality and expressiveness was functional for the children, the parents, and especially the society. It prevented role duplication and was efficient, since society did not have to train everyone in all possible roles. Bakan, however, in line with feminist doctrine, suggested that the viability of both the individual and the society was dependent on the successful integration of agency and communion. In our terms, Bakan argued for androgyny while Parsons and Bales argued for sex typing.

Irrespective of theoretical debates over the best approach for society, the fact is that most individual children are taught, and learn, in line with Parsons and Bales' prescription of specialization along the axis of sex. Not only parents, but others in the child's environment provide anticipatory socialization that helps the child develop an appropriate gender role. Every day on television, in many of his kiddy books, and even outside in the real world the child sees that men and women, boys and girls are different. He is exposed to the anticipatory socialization of others. Peers call the boy a sissy if he is not tough. Adults comment on the sweet, charming, or neat little girl. People certainly act differently toward a child depending on whether it is a boy or a girl.

When the child starts school, he is exposed in a more continual fashion to feedback from peers. Whether teachers provide appropriate gender role training has been debated. Certainly we know that the child with inappropriate gender role is ostracized by his peers. A boy who continually plays with dolls and refuses to play with trucks is left out of activities with other boys. Girls, too, will ostracize him. In essence, he is seen as an oddity—he has not been enculturated into societal norms.

The components of gender role are further intensified as the child approaches puberty. During the prepubertal years from seven to twelve, the child continually encounters new dimensions of external regulation in the school and peer group (e.g. males and females use different bathrooms and may have recess in different yards). Gender roles are imitated, played at, and acted out, not only in play, but also in real life.

It is also noticeable that adolescents prefer the company of their same-sex peers, in an effort to confirm their own identity. At any rate, the child's experience with behaviors typical for his sex is increased in these same-sex peer groups, and the behavior of the opposite sex is avoided. This period provides the framework for a more secure sexual identity through gender role learning and rehearsal. And it sets the stage for the heterosexual interchange in adolescence. If all goes well, the child emerges from this period with a sense of sexual identity strong enough to withstand the decisive period of adolescence.

Adolescence

At adolescence, the child begins the path to adulthood and leaves behind his primary dependence on the childhood configuration of the family. Adolescence begins biologically. Long before emotional contradictions arise in the course of growth towards adulthood, hormonal changes begin to work their effects on the body. For the girl, menstruation is a sign of womanhood. For the boy, the signs occur more gradually and include increased growth of the body, a gradual change in voice, and facial hair.

Partly because of these and other changes that affect the body image, the adolescent's most pertinent problem, and one under which many of his other problems can be subsumed, is the question, "Who am I?"

One can see, then, the importance of having as stable a sexual identity as possible as one comes into adolescence. Nature herself reinforces the developing sexual identity with different biological characteristics for each sex. The mores and cultural expectations of the child's environment continue to provide a frame of reference for his specific gender role. And, even in adolescence, the attitudes and behavior of parents, peers, and others who are meaningful to the individual provide training, feedback, and modeling of the appropriate gender role.

Early adolescence is a period of rapid growth and major hormonal change. As a result, the young person must be prepared to accept a changed physical self and, consequently, a new self-image. This stage includes the turmoil associated with the often dramatic physical changes. Rapid mood swings, angry rebellion against parents and adults, and a tendency to be with members of the same sex are all evident during this period.

Later adolescence provides new pressures but also new opportunities for release of emotional tension and for sexual identity support through sexual activities. One of the most important tasks of the late adolescent is to integrate aspects of his personality into a stabilized, unique, separate identity that can be confirmed and supported by society.

Weaving between parental and societal expectations and his own feelings, the adolescent turns to his peer group for comparison. He does not question the wisdom of having his personality crystalized from the outside inward. He first tries to find himself in comparison with others and then tries to acquire confidence that he is who he seems to be.

As the adolescent becomes more aware of his surroundings, movement is made toward acknowledgment of the opposite sex. With the first awakenings of sexual desire, the adolescent gradually moves on to heterosexual relationships. Boys and girls begin to pay more attention to one another. However, due to the young people's self-preoccupation, deep emotional involvements with the opposite sex are rare, and there is usually a superficial, gamelike quality to heterosexual interaction at this stage. It is almost like the play behavior of the child. The adolescent is "trying out his wings" in the area of heterosexual relations, which is an area related to gender role.

Adolescents frequently feel uncertain about their sexual identity. They become frightened over aspects of themselves that they fear contradict their own image of masculinity and femininity. Many of these people do not feel that they clearly belong to any one sex. The popular image of a typical process of adolescent identity formation is that of an intense period of identity confusion or acute identity crisis characterized by marked emotional turmoil and upheaval. Virtually all adolescents experience some degree of identity confusion, and still, virtually all of them to some degree consolidate their sense of sexual identity and self-identity.

I have briefly sketched some of the factors that result in the development of a sexual identity including gender identity and gender role. In so doing, I have given the impression that there are phases that succeed one another. However, this is untrue. These phases overlap, and in virtually no case may the person be said to be progressing smoothly from one phase to another. The individual normally fluctuates back and forth, testing out himself and his environment in various ways.

Hence the male child might try on some girl's clothing to see what it is like, and then again in adoles-

cence might don female apparel for sexual excitement.
This does not necessarily mean that the individual's
sexual identity is in peril. It probably is merely a normal
attempt to try out different alternatives and make sure,
so to speak, that he is doing the right thing. If such
opposite gender role behavior persists, however, it is an
indicator that something is awry with the sexual
identity.

Also, the late adolescent might slip back into his own
sex-peer group or his family for support and reassurance
while breaking away from heterosexual involvement.
Such a temporary setback can be viewed as normal and
to many may serve as a necessary respite from what is
seen as a frightening situation. However, the thirty-year-
old who is still anchored in his original family, afraid to
venture into a heterosexual relationship, may be seen as
having sexual identity problems.

This chapter has emphasized the relevance of specific key events and interactions in the development and
acquisition of sexual identity. It should be recognized
that the impact of some of the periods of development has
not been extensively studied. The bulk of both research
and theorizing has concentrated in and emphasized the
earliest years of development. The area of preadoles-
cence, though of potential importance, has certainly not
received the attention it deserves. In fact it has been
called the "latency period" by some because it was once
believed that little was going on during this period.

Further, this chapter has been based largely on what
could be called a social-learning view of sexual identity.
Other theories do exist, but I feel that the framework
presented is the most plausible and most easily
explained. This model is sketched in diagrammatic form
in Figure 2. The model involves role expectations that
lead to role sending, which in turn leads to role receiving.
The process culminates in a behavioral response to the
received role. In reality, it is difficult to determine a
beginning or an endpoint to this process, for it is all

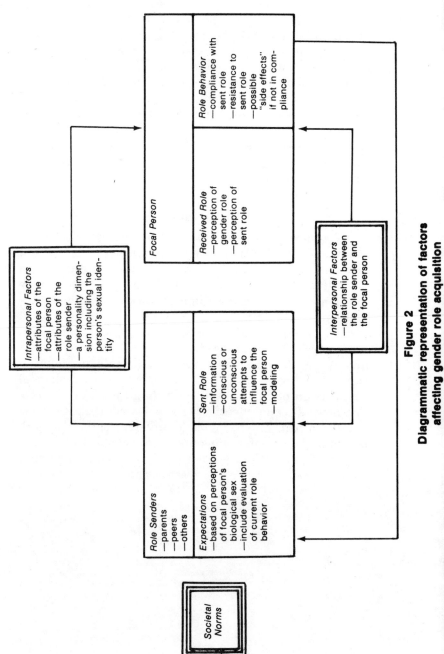

Figure 2
**Diagrammatic representation of factors
affecting gender role acquisition**

Intrapersonal Factors
—attributes of the focal person
—attributes of the role sender
—a personality dimension including the person's sexual identity

Focal Person

Received Role
—perception of gender role
—perception of sent role

Role Behavior
—compliance with sent role
—resistance to sent role
—possible "side effects" if not in compliance

Interpersonal Factors
—relationship between the role sender and the focal person

Role Senders
—parents
—peers
—others

Sent Role
—information
—conscious or unconscious attempts to influence the focal person
—modeling

Expectations
—based on perceptions of focal person's biological sex
—include evaluation of current role behavior

Societal Norms

33

occurring simultaneously for all the specifics of gender
role. The model is, necessarily, a simplified one. The
actual acquisition of gender roles is a complex phenomenon. But, to the best of our knowledge, this simplified
model is what is happening throughout life. Subsequent
chapters will deal with some of the problems that snarl
up this process and some of the environmental situations
that can affect this role acquisition model. But prior to
this I shall discuss the measurement of sexual identity.
This is a topic of importance to scientists and of interest
to the average reader.

Summary

The development of sexual identity begins at birth.
Males and females are given different types of names and
different colors of clothing and are treated differently.
Even though many parents believe they treat their male
and female children the same, studies have shown that
mothers's and fathers's actions and reactions toward
their children depend on the sex of the child. Studies with
human pseudohermaphrodites demonstrate that almost
anyone can be raised as a male or a female and develop
this attributed sexual identity regardless of biological
sex. It is proposed that the overriding force in the establishment of sexual identity is social learning, that is, how
one is trained. The basic model involves both communication to the person of his appropriate gender role behavior and feedback to the person of his current behavior.
This process is ongoing throughout life.

III.
The Measurement of Sexual Identity

In Chapter 1, I delineated the meaning of sexual identity. I followed this chapter with a chapter on how such sexual identity develops in a person as a result of environmental influences. It is the purpose of the present chapter to discuss how one can measure sexual identity.

While the delineation of the meaning of sexual identity is essential for common understanding, it is but a preliminary step for the research psychologist. What must next be ascertained is how to determine or measure the sexual identity of any individual. Note that I am again using the blanket term sexual identity, which includes both gender identity and gender role.

It has been a maxim in experimental psychology that everything that exists, exists in some quantity. And, if it exists in some quantity, it can be measured. The measurement of sexual identity has been such a problem area that some might think sexual identity does not exist. Such a statement is nonsense. Sexual identity does exist, and it can be measured. The difficulty with traditional methods of measuring sexual identity has lain in the method whereby the measuring instrument was constructed.

Designing Sexual Identity Tests

The traditional method of sexual identity test construction consists of a maximum of four steps. The first is to select a pool of items to be examined. The selection process might have some theoretical basis or simply be random. Second, groups of males and females are tested for their response to the items, and it is determined how the responses of males and females differ. The differences form the key to the determination of sexual identity distinction. The third step has actually been optional to many tests. It consists of testing a group of homosexuals, normally only males. This step is considered a validation because homosexuals are supposed to be a group with sexual identity problems and therefore should respond to the test items differently than do heterosexual males. The fourth step, which is often considered a formality, is to take the test just devised, give it to another group of males and females, and hope that it differentiates them. This last step is known as cross-validation.

The following is an example of the procedure just described. Ask 100 males and 100 females whether they prefer blue or red. You may find that 75 percent of the males like red and 80 percent of the females choose blue. Then ask male homosexuals the same question. You may find that 60 percent of them prefer blue. (Actually, for validation purposes, they need not respond so much like females as they have to respond differently from most males.) Then ask another group of males and females the question. If you find a similar distribution of color preference as in the first group of males and females, you have designed a one item test of sexual identity—or, at least, so it would seem.

There are actually some very real problems with such a method of test construction. The first is that not every item to which the sexes respond differently (the basic criterion for item inclusion) is an indicator of sexual identity. For example, instead of asking color preference, suppose we asked, "Do your genitals protrude more than half an inch from your abdomen?" Provided that everyone knew what the question meant, most males would respond affirmatively and virtually all females would respond negatively. Yet, while this is an item of sex differentiation, it only indicates biological sex and is certainly not an indicator of sexual identity.

In fact, even transsexual males, who by definition have a sexual identity reversal, respond affirmatively to the question, provided it is asked prior to a sex change operation. This illustration is an exaggeration of the problem, but it is at least a clear way to demonstrate that a sex difference is not necessarily a sexual identity indicator.

The typical inclusion of a male homosexual group as a validation criterion is poor for two reasons. First, as noted in Chapter 1, all aspects of a homosexual's sexual identity need not be reversed. True, for the specific "Would you prefer sex with a male or a female," a homosexual has, by the definition of homosexuality, a gender role adoption of the opposite sex. But this may be the only specific in which his gender role is reversed. Hence, as a validation criterion for sexual identity research, homosexuals are a poor sample to use.

The second problem with using male homosexuals is that homosexuals in general probably have more anxiety about themselves than do heterosexuals, and this anxiety may affect their responses more than does sexual identity per se. To decide whether differential responses of homosexuals stem from sexual identity disorders or from anxiety, one would need to examine both male and female homosexuals. For example, let us say that heterosexual males and females are asked to throw a ball into a basket ten feet away. Males would do better than females. Next, homosexual males are asked to participate in the experiment. They know that you know of their homosexuality. That is why they are there. Since there is still a stigmatization associated with homosexuality, they are very anxious about why you would want to see someone who is a homosexual. This anxiety may cause them to do poorly at shooting baskets. In a traditional test of sexual identity, this outcome would be sufficient to conclude that basket shooting is an aspect of sexual identity. Yet, these same homosexuals, on a basketball court, with no one aware of their homosexuality, might do just as well as the heterosexual males tested or even better. In fact, such an unobtrusive measure might be one way around this problem. An easier way would be to ask homosexual females to also shoot baskets. If their performance is also poor, one should accept the anxiety hypothesis. However, if the female homosexuals' performance is better than the female heterosexuals' performance, then basket shooting could be an indicator of sexual identity. Nonetheless, it remains true that homosexuals are a poor validation group because homosexuality is independent of sexual identity reversal.

The tests of sexual identity provided up to now included only one specific. Actual tests of sexual identity include many different items. A person could be asked to give an association to each of seventy words, describe himself with sixty different adjectives, find hidden figures in twelve different designs. These multiple-item tests many times present another problem: it is difficult to pinpoint which aspect of sexual identity the test addresses. Many of these tests tap more than one such aspect. For instance, one test, the California Psychological Inventory (CPI), includes a femininity scale that confounds gender role preference ("I would like to be a nurse") with gender role adoption ("I get excited easily"). As research in sexual identity becomes more precise, tests that confound various aspects will become less and less useful.

These basic problems, however, should not put off anyone who might be interested in developing a sexual identity test. There are resolutions to these problems. A more valid approach to sexual identity test construction will now be presented. The differentiation of males and females is a necessary first step in sexual identity test development. So the first two steps of traditional test construction remain the same: (1) selection of a pool of items to be examined, and (2) differentiation of males and females in their responses to these items.

The third step still involves a validation criterion, but we now have a better group against which to validate our found sex differences. That group consists of transsexuals. Both biological males and females should be used for validation purposes in the transsexual group. If our items reflect sexual identity, we should find dissimilarities between nontranssexual males and females, nontranssexual and transsexual males, nontranssexual and transsexual females, and transsexual males and females. We should find similarities between nontranssexual females and transsexual males and between nontranssexual males and transsexual females. In short, transsexual males and nontranssexual females should be similar to each other and different from transsexual females and nontranssexual males, who should also resemble each other. If the results correlate as described, we can be fairly certain that we are tapping certain aspects of sexual identity. But the more similar the transsexual males and females, the less sure we can be that the test is one of sexual identity and the more plausible is the explanation that anxiety or some other feature of transsexualism per se is producing the effect.

Now I should like to address the problem of which aspect of sexual identity is being measured. Gender role adoption, preference, and ability generally are easily distinguishable, and any one test should try to include only one of these aspects. It may be more difficult to distinguish between an item that reflects gender identity and one that indicates gender role.

For distinguishing between gender identity and gender role, the only apparent recourse is to administer the validated test items to homosexual males and females. We have already noted that nonpatient homosexuals are generally satisfied in their biological sex but that they adopt, to different degrees, the role of the opposite sex. One could perhaps select a group of homosexuals who seemed to emulate a great many qualities of the opposite sex, give them the test, and compare their scores or results with those of nontranssexual, nonhomosexual males and females. Items that did not differentiate the homosexuals from the control males and females could be said to reflect gender identity. Gender role adoption would be indicated by items receiving one set of answers from homosexual males and control group females and a different set of answers by homosexual females and control group males.

This procedure, of course, is not as clear-cut as one might like. It also is dependent on how much gender role reversal the homosexuals are experiencing. We might wish to include only those homosexual males who preferred to be sexually penetrated rather than to penetrate, who wore female clothing, who had consciously adopted feminine mannerisms. who wore makeup, who stayed home and kept house while their lovers went out to work, and who did not actively seek out sexual encounters. Female homosexuals we would want to test would have many of the opposite characteristics. Such individuals may be difficult to find.

This entire new approach to sexual identity test construction is overall very difficult and time-consuming. For example, access to transsexual populations is difficult for the average researcher. Even individuals affiliated with gender identity clinics often report research on transsexuals whose number is very small (often less than ten). Female transsexuals are even more difficult to find than male transsexuals. Needless to say, therefore, such a test construction is, and should be, a massive effort. It is unfortunate that while the theory of sexual identity is becoming more exact, sexual identity test construction is becoming less and less rigorous.

Let us compare, for example, the first sexual identity test, developed in 1936 by Lewis Terman and Catherine Cox Miles, with Sandra Bem's Sex Role Inventory (the BSRI) which was developed in 1974. The Terman-Miles M-F Test consists of seven different exercises: Word Association, Inkblot Association, Information, Interests, Introversion, Emotional and Ethical Attitudes, and Opinions. Obviously, Terman and Miles believed in the multidimensionality of sexual identity, and low correlations among results of the separate exercises support that notion. The BSRI, on the other hand, consists of one task: adjectival self-description. Further, Terman and Miles developed two separate forms of their test, each complete with seven exercises. There is only one form of the BSRI.

Terman and Miles examined how test results varied with such factors as age, occupation, educational level, university major, and homosexual involvement. They further correlated scores obtained on their test with the individual's intelligence and scholarship. This was done for both forms of their test, with many different groups of people from across the country. The BSRI, on the other hand, was standardized only on university students who were all residing within 100 miles of each other in California. Little attention was paid to the effect that variables other than gender could have had on the test scores.

There are other differences between the developmental procedures of these two tests, and in almost every case the older test has the edge. Bem's test was used for comparison only because it is the most recently developed sexual identity test I know of; just about any other sexual identity test would also be inferior to the Terman-Miles M-F Test in terms of test development.

In fact, despite the age of the Terman-Miles M-F Test (it is now over forty years old), William Piper and I were able to demonstrate, using the first three exercises, that the test can still differentiate males and females (LaTorre and Piper 1978). The rigor that went into developing the test must surely account for a great part of the test's continuing validity. Furthermore, Paitich (1973) uses the test to distinguish transsexuals from nontranssexuals.

Behavioral Tests

Most of the tests of sexual identity that have just been discussed have been paper-and-pencil, self-report inventories. An individual may be asked to describe himself in some way on a number of items or to give personal responses that are not direct self-descriptions. However, one other type of test, not yet explored sufficiently, may hold great promise for at least the measurement of gender role. This is the behavioral test.

Many paper and pencil inventories, especially the self-report types (e.g. "How aggressive are you? Would you like the work of a librarian?"), are transparent and susceptible to faking. Transparency means that a person can guess what the test is all about. Consider the following list of questions: "Are you bothered by hearing weird noises that do not exist? Do you often see things that are not there? Do you have trouble thinking? Have you seen beings from other planets? Is everybody in the world trying to kill you?" Such a line of questioning would lead a person to suspect that the test was trying to determine his sanity. In this respect the test is transparent. Most people know that they should answer each question in the negative if they do not want their sanity questioned. Therefore, they would be capable of "faking" the test— that is, giving untrue responses to deliberately influence the results.

Transparency and faking may seem related, but they can be independent. That we know the purpose of a test does not mean we can fake the results. We know that an arithmetic test is measuring our mathematical abilities, but this knowledge does not mean we can fake doing well (although we could fake doing poorly). On the other hand, the fact that we can give untrue responses on a test does not mean that we know the purpose of the test.

Transparency and especially faking are problems associated with paper and pencil tests. Behavioral tests do not question the individual but rather observe him in a situation or a number of situations. We could watch an individual's behavior and rate him accordingly on a checklist of male and female items. Such a behavioral list has been developed by a group of workers at Upstate Medical Center in New York and at Harvard Medical School (Schatzberg et al. 1975). Their checklist includes observations of speech, gait, posture and tonus, mouth movements, upper face and eyes, hand and torso gestures, body type, and body narcissism. Characteristics defined as feminine might include speaking with soft tones, lisping or using a sibilant *s*, taking small mincing steps and rubbing the thighs together while walking, sitting with one leg tucked under the body and displaying a limp wrist; displaying the tongue and smiling seductively; fluttering the eyelashes and maintaining prolonged eye contact; rocking the pelvis while sitting and making an excessive number of wrist movements; having a pear-shaped body and appearing younger than stated age; preening the hair and stroking the head or mustache.

This test can be falsified, but it should not be transparent because a person need not know that he is even being observed for that purpose. In fact, the observation could be so unobtrusive that a person need not know he is being observed at all. We know that Tom Sawyer, when dressed as a girl, was discovered, not because he gave inappropriate verbal responses, but because he displayed a masculine behavior: he tried to catch something in his lap by closing his legs rather than by opening them.

Another type of behavioral test would be to place an individual in a room wherein there are objects of interest primarily to males or females and to observe which objects attract his attention. In a waiting room, for example, it could be observed whether the individual picks up *Playboy, Mechanix Illustrated,* or *Argosy,* or whether he reads *Playgirl, Cosmopolitan,* or *True Romances.*

Unfortunately, few such behavioral studies of sexual identity have been made. Use of the behavioral measure, we would hope, will come into vogue in the future. It is much more accurate than self-reports. Actions speak louder than words.

Abilities Tests

Another type of test that could reveal sexual identity is the abilities test. An example would be shooting baskets. Males and females adopt different abilities. Many or most of these are learned because they are part of the individual's sexual identity. "I am a boy. Because I am a boy, I like and want to do boy things, not girl things. Shooting baskets is a boy thing; therefore, I shall learn to shoot baskets."

One problem with abilities testing is that the results, more than with some other kinds of tests, can be manifestations of simple sex differences. Men can run faster and farther than women (given equal training) because males can take more air into their lungs and have greater musculoskeletal adaptibility. The abilities that are sex-linked and purely biological can easily be distinguished from those resulting from psychological differences by using the transsexual validation group.

For example, at McGill University and the Montreal General Hospital, groups of transsexuals and nontranssexuals were tested on a number of abilities (LaTorre, Gossmann, and Piper 1976). It was found that transsexual males and nontranssexual females took longer to find simple figures hidden in complex designs than did nontranssexual males. Therefore, disembedding figures seems to be an ability that is useful for sexual identity measurement. In the same study, the manual dexterity of males (both transsexual and nontranssexual) was poorer than the manual dexterity of nontranssexual females. Hence, manual dexterity seems to be a biological difference and is not a good sexual identity measure.

Abilities testing for sexual identity measurement has the advantage that a person cannot fake an ability he does not have. It is, of course, possible to appear less able than one actually is, but people usually try to make themselves appear better, not worse. Also, the transparency of abilities testing for sexual identity measurement is nearly zero. How would anyone know that finding simple figures in complex designs is an indication of one's sexual identity? As a result, such measurements need not be unobtrusive.

Body Image Tests for Gender Identity

Another type of measurement that I should like to discuss deals with body image. Such measurements are particularly important since body image is so intimately linked with the development of gender identity. As such, the measurements may be the only such tests we currently possess that assess gender identity as opposed to gender role. Several tests based in one way or another upon body image have been used as sexual identity measures.

One of the most common projective tests associated with gender identity is the Draw-a-Person (DAP) test. An individual is first asked simply to draw a person, and then is asked to draw a person of the opposite sex to the figure drawn first. One assumption of this test is that the individual will project himself into the drawing. It has been consistently demonstrated that 80 percent to 100 percent of males and 60 percent to 80 percent of females draw a person of their own sex first. In fact, the assumption of self-projection has been supported in a study in which females made drawings of females and also were photographed (Apfeldorf and Smith 1966). Sixty individuals compared the photographs with the drawings and were able to match a drawing with the photograph of its maker at a better than 1 in 100 level of chance. That is, the pairing of drawings with photographs was not a random procedure.

One of the problems with this technique is that it does not take into account gradations of identification. That is, a male figure is drawn first by about the same percentages of two groups of males—those with a secure male self-definition and those with an insecure male self-definition. Therefore, a scale was developed to measure degrees of sexual differentiation by comparing the male and female figures an individual draws (Swensen 1955). The Sexual Differentiation Scale is a nine point measure with scores ranging from little or no sexual differentiation between the two figures to excellent differentiation between the two. However, there is still some question as to the extent that drawing ability affects the pictorial representation of sexual differentiation.

Another possible gender identity test is the Body Parts Satisfaction Test. An individual rates his satisfaction or dissatisfaction with twenty different body parts. Some parts are designated as masculine, some as feminine, and the remainder as non-sex related. Males are normally more satisfied with their bodies than are females. Females are believed to be less satisfied with the female body parts and males with the male body parts.

Another test that presumably taps gender identity is the Franck and Rosen (1949) Drawing Completion (DC) Test. The DC Test consists of thirty-six incomplete drawings that the individual completes any way he chooses. This test is theoretically linked to body image because males tend to draw angular shapes with protrusions while females draw more circular patterns with openings and internal embellishments.

In addition to completing drawings in a sex-typed manner, an individual tends to prefer figures that represent salient aspects of his or her own body. Hence males are known to prefer angular figures, upright figures, and figures that depict some sort of penetration (e.g. an arrow through a square). Females prefer circular figures, figures with openings, and slanted figures. Normally such a test (e.g. the Figure Preference Test) is given as a forced choice test so that an individual must choose one and only one of two or possibly several alternatives.

A behavioral test dealing with body image could be mirror gazing. It is believed that this behavior develops from a concern about the body image. A person stares into a mirror in an attempt to find a clearer picture of his or her own body. The observation of an individual from behind a one-way mirror could consist simply of counting the number of times or the total amount of time the person looks at himself in the mirror. We could hypothesize that, the greater the number of times or the longer the time spent, the more the individual is concerned with his body image and therefore his sexual identity.

An abilities test reflecting body image could be the Embedded Figures Test. As was mentioned before, this test requires that the individual find a simple figure within a complex design. The only problem is that, in all the other tests discussed, females prefer to deal with the internal aspects of the figure. Yet, in the Embedded Figures Test, females have more difficulty than males in dealing with internal aspects (wherein lies the embedded figure). Perhaps it could be the female's difficulty in dealing with internal aspects that makes her preoccupied with those aspects. This preoccupation makes her embellish internal aspects of figures when asked to complete drawings because it gives her a sense of mastery or control over something with which she has a difficult time. This relationship, however, remains unclear and further research is needed.

Gender Role Adoption Tests

Most sexual identity tests seem to be largely measures of gender role adoption (albeit several confound adoption with gender role preference). Such tests are numerous. Some of the more common are the Minnesota

Multiphasic Personality Inventory (MMPI) Masculinity-Femininity (M-F) scale; the CPI Femininity scale, parts of the Terman-Miles M-F Test; and the BSRI. To give an idea of these tests to the reader unfamiliar with them, a gender role adoption test similar to the BSRI is given in Table 2. There are numerous such tests available to the clinician or researcher. One hopes that behavioral and ability tests of gender role adoption will be implemented in the near future.

Table 2
Sample gender role adoption test

Directions: For each of the adjectival descriptions listed below, indicate on the 7-point scale how well each describes you. Place a circle around the appropriate X.

	Never or Almost Never True	Sometimes True, Sometimes Not True	Always or Almost Always True
1. I usually give up easily in an argument.	X X X X	X X	X
2. I think things through carefully before I act.	X X X X	X X	X
3. I am shy when I meet new people.	X X X X	X X	X
4. I like to take part in many different sports.	X X X X	X X	X
5. I like to be cuddled.	X X X X	X X	X
6. I feel masculine.	X X X X	X X	X
7. I fall for untrue stories.	X X X X	X X	X
8. In a group of people I usually end up making the decisions.	X X X X	X X	X

4.2

9. I could spend all day playing with small children.

10. I usually try to further myself in everything I do.

11. I am willing to listen to people who are sad or depressed.

12. I need nobody's help but my own.

13. I do not swear.

14. I will defend what I believe in.

15. I feel feminine.

16. I let no one push me around.

17. I am usually cheerful.

18. I make up my mind easily.

19. I will do more for someone if that person says nice things to me.

20. I enjoy competition.

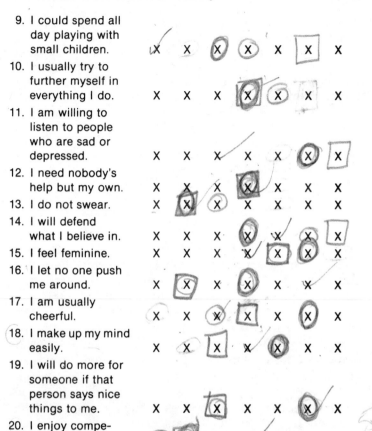

Note: This is an unstandardized test presented for illustrative purposes. Results obtained from this test should be considered suspect.

Scoring: Each of the twenty items is given a score of 1 through 7, depending on which X is circled. If the X farthest to the left in a sequence is circled, the score is 1 point. The next X to the right scores 2 points, the next 3 points, and so on. The X at the right of the sequence has a value of 7 points.

First, add up all the points for all the even-numbered items and divide the total by 10. (If some even-numbered items were not answered, the total should be divided by the number of items that were answered). The result is the masculinity average score. Next, do the same for all the odd-numbered items. The result is the feminity average score. Now, subtract the femininity score *from* the masculinity score. If the difference score is equal to or greater than +1, you have attained a clearly masculine score. If the difference score is greater than +0.5 but less than +1, your score is classified as slightly masculine. If the difference score is less than or equal to -1, you have a clearly feminine score. If it is less than -0.5 but greater than -1, your score is slightly feminine. Scores from -0.5 to +0.5 can be labeled androgynous.

Gender Role Preference Tests

There are few tests of gender role preference. One of the most used is the Role Preference Test, in which an individual chooses which of two possible roles he would prefer to play in a drama or pageant. This test presents a number of pairs of roles, each pair consisting of one male and one female role (e.g. devil or witch). The more male choices are made, the more the individual is said to have a male gender role preference; the more female alternatives are chosen, the more the person is said to have a female gender role preference.

Direct questioning (either overt or clandestine) seems to be the only way to assess gender role preference. Behavioral and abilities tests cannot adequately tap preference. The fact that one behaves a certain way does not mean that one prefers to behave that way. The fact that a male does not have the ability to score a goal every time he gets the puck does not mean he prefers not to score each time.

Gender Role Ability Tests

Gender role ability has probably been the most neglected aspect of sexual identity, both in theory and in test development. This aspect of sexual identity should actually be quite accessible to testing by both behavioral and abilities tests. To truly test gender role ability, as opposed to adoption, it is almost essential to set up the following condition. Inform the person of the purpose of the test. Tell this person that it is a test in which males and females respond differently. Next tell him that he should respond as masculinely or as femininely as possible. In this way, you can find out, not what he does, but what he is capable of doing. In a true abilities test a person must go all out and do the best he can—in this case, in as masculine or feminine a manner as possible.

Because the areas of gender role preference and gender role ability have been only sparingly dealt with in the literature, these areas are ripe for future scrutinization.

Dimensions of Sexual Identity Measurement

The final aspect of sexual identity measurement that I should like to discuss is one that was first mentioned in Chapter I: the debate whether masculinity and femininity are endpoints of a single dimension or whether they are independent constructs. As previously stated, I believe that any one specific *is* independent of one's masculinity or femininity on another specific.

In terms of measurement, however, it really makes little difference. Most sexual identity tests use a summative score that places a person somewhere along one dimension with masculinity and femininity as endpoints on that dimension. The nearer the person's score is to one endpoint (e.g. masculinity), the farther it is from the other (e.g. femininity). Bem (1974) developed a test, similar to that in Table 2, that boasted separate masculinity and femininity scales. These scales were shown to be independent. Hence, a person high in masculinity could score high, moderate, or low in femininity. Traditional tests do not provide such independent scoring. However, even Bem uses something similar to a summative score, for she compares the masculinity and the femininity scores against each other and transforms them into a single standardized score that, again, places the person on one continuum with masculinity at one end and femininity at the other; the term 'androgyny' is used to label the midpoint of the continuum.

Heilbrun (1976) also reported that he could obtain independent masculinity and femininity scales from his traditional-type test, the Adjective Check List. However, when an individual's score obtained by this method was compared with his score from the traditional method, a significant positive correlation emerged.

I took a small sample of Terman-Miles Information subtests and determined masculinity and femininity scales that were statistically independent from each other. However, the score obtained by comparing the masculinity and the femininity scale scores was highly correlated to the score obtained by the summative method.

Theoretically, one can view masculinity and femininity independently. But, in terms of test scores, it seems to make little difference whether one obtains a difference score by comparing independent masculine and feminine scales or uses a traditional summative score.

Summary

The measurement of sexual identity rests on the following premise: A difference between the sexes on their responses to any test item can be taken as an indicator of sex typing, masculinity-femininity, or sexual identity. This operational criterion leaves much to be desired. For example, a validation group of transsexuals should also be tested. If their responses are congruent with their biological sex, and not their sexual identity, then the test is purely a measure that differentiates biological males from biological females. Such a test does not tap sexual identity. Traditional tests also rely heavily on self-reports, which can be faked and are often transparent. Behavioral and abilities testing promise to more accurately tap sexual identity. Finally, while masculinity and femininity seem to be independent constructs, it makes little difference whether one uses a traditional summative score or a difference score obtained by comparing independent masculinity and femininity scales, since the two methods of scoring are correlated.

IV.
Sexual Identity and Psychopathology

Sexual identity problems have been linked to many types of psychological problems. Around the turn of the century, the sexual identity of paranoid schizophrenics was questioned. Von Krafft-Ebing, author of *Psychopathia Sexualis* (1933), noted that many paranoid schizophrenics experienced delusions of sex change. He labeled this phenomenon *metamorphosis paranoica sexualis*.

The alert clinician can detect this same problem in modern-day populations. I once interviewed a middle-aged woman who believed, among other apparent delusions, that her family was putting testosterone (male sex hormone) into her food at home because they wanted to turn her into a man. This particular symptom may have been precipitated by changes in her body brought about by menopause.

Sigmund Freud (1925), in his analysis of the Schreber case, proposed a theoretical explanation for the linkage

between sexual identity problems and paranoid schizophrenia. The case concerned a man who beleived that he
would give birth to a new mankind and that the sun
would be the father. Freud's theory, simply explained, is
that paranoid schizophrenics have a homosexual orientation or that, in the case of males, the female aspect of the
personality dominates or tries to dominate the person.
The opposite would be true of female paranoid schizophrenics. Freud believed that everyone is born with both
male and female potentials. In Freud's time, homosexuality was an even more unacceptable behavior than it is today. As a result, the individual transformed the feeling "I
want to have homosexual contacts with others" to a
belief that "others want to have homosexual contacts
with me." This alleviated any guilt the person might feel
about having homosexual thoughts or desires. However,
this new belief could not legitimately be held if others did
not make any sexual advances or overtures; so even the
transformed wish had to be transformed. The belief that
"others want to have homosexual contacts with me," was
transmitted into the conviction that "others want to
harm me." Certainly, in daily life there are enough
instances in which one could rationalize the veracity of
the last transformation. Consider the following: "The
government is watching all of us . . . my wife is trying to
poison me through her cooking . . . people keep trying to
run me over."

In essence, Freud suggested that paranoia or paranoid schizophrenia (the labels given to the illnesses of
those who think they are important people such as Hitler
or Napoleon, who believe they are being persecuted, or
who are extremely jealous or suspicious) is a defense
against a homosexual wish. This theory has actually
been a topic for research since the first sexual identity
test was developed in 1936. A study published in 1938
compared the scores obtained on this test by three
different groups: normal male and female controls, homosexual males, and both paranoid and paranoid schizo-

phrenic male patients (Page and Warkentin 1938). The scores of male paranoid patients were slightly more feminine than were the scores of control males. On the other hand, the paranoid patients were considerably more masculine than either a group of "passive" male homosexuals or a group of control females. In fact, the difference between paranoid males and homosexual males was eight to nine times greater than the difference between paranoid males and control males. And the difference between paranoid males and normal females was sixteen to seventeen times greater than the difference between paranoid and normal control males. Therefore, this study gave little support to Freud's theory.

The idea that paranoia is associated with a repressed homosexual wish, or impaired sexual identity orientation, has persisted for almost three-fourths of a century, albeit it has met with much criticism. This is such a debated issue that two different individuals reviewing much of the same literature arrived at different conclusions (Lester 1975; Wolowitz 1971). Overall, it would appear that there is modest, but not conclusive, support for the hypothesis that paranoia is associated with a slightly feminine sexual identity for males.

The evidence on female paranoids is very sparse. What there is suggests no such sexual identity reversal. For example, despite Freud's theory, it has been shown that the persecutors in female paranoid schizophrenics' delusions are usually males. If female paranoids were also defending against homosexual desires, their persecutors would be females.

One might like to propose that the female goes through an extra stage wherein she transforms, not only the behavior, but also the sex of the other person. Her thought would thus progress, "I want to have sex with females . . . Females want to have sex with me . . . Females want to harm me . . . Males want to harm me." This could make sense: it is correct that males do more harm than females. However, this extra step makes the process considerably more complicated. It would be much more efficient, and it would even make more sense, for the female to rationalize, "I want to have sex with females . . . females want to have sex with me . . . males want to have sex with me."

Differences such as these have led at least one researcher (May 1970) to suggest that there is no such a thing as a female paranoid schizophrenic. May's research actually dealt with power (aggression and assertion), which has been shown to be a sexual identity specific. It has been demonstrated that male paranoid schizophrenics have more anxiety about power than do normal males. However, female paranoid schizophrenics have no more anxiety on the subject than normal females.

While the sexual identity of at least male paranoid schizophrenics may be less appropriate than is that of normal males, there is almost contradictory evidence regarding the idea that paranoia is a defense against homosexual impulses. Under Freud's theory, the paranoid delusion covers up a homosexual wish that is totally unacceptable to the individual. If effective, this delusion helps prevent the individual from having homosexual thoughts, fantasies, and, especially, behavior. Yet, there is ample information available to demonstrate that there is actually a high incidence of homosexuality within the paranoid schizophrenic group. Homosexuality within this group does not contradict the presence of sexual identity difficulties, but it does argue against paranoid delusions being a *defense against* homosexuality. Nonetheless, Freud has made a significant contribution. Although the specific theory would appear to be inaccurate, he did point out a possible general area of difficulty that could lead to paranoid symptoms.

Modern Theories

The next major theorist to discuss the relationship between sexual identity and psychopathology was Alfred Adler (1956; 1964), who proposed . a slightly more encompassing theory. Like Freud, Adler believed that everyone has, inherent in his being, both maleness and femaleness. The healthy individual is able to separate the two and adopt the one appropriate for his biological sex. On the other hand, the essence of neurosis is a double life: the neurotic's psyche partakes of both masculine and feminine aspects, which remain in conflict with each other. Hence, the neurotic is involved in a constant struggle between his masculine and feminine beings. Adler therefore listed sexual identity uncertainty as a primary precursor to psychopathology in general.

As a matter of fact, numerous research studies have supported the hypothesis that sexual identity uncertainty, reversal, confusion, or alienation is associated with psychopathology. One of the most recent studies explored Adler's idea that the neurotic was involved in a 'double life' regarding his sexual identity. LaTorre and Gregoire (1977) administered the BSRI (the androgyny test discussed in Chapter 3) to three groups of university students. These groups were solicited: (1) while waiting to see a doctor for medical reasons at a university health service; (2) while waiting to see a doctor for psychological reasons at the same health service; and (3) at large university meeting places. It was found that students seeking psychiatric treatment were more androgynous than students in the other two groups. In fact, significant differences between males and females, apparent in the two control groups, were absent in the psychiatric group.

Previous research studies also support the notion that neurotics and psychotics (either hospitalized or seeking some sort of psychiatric care) had difficulties with their sexual identity. Typically, they attained sexual identity scores less appropriate for their biological sex than did a group not receiving psychiatric attention.

However, there are problems with defining mental health or illness in terms of mental health care received. One of the basic problems is that so-called normal controls (defined as those not obtaining psychiatric aid) could actually include some very pathological individuals who have not (for reasons such as fear of social ridicule or lack of money) sought out the psychiatric aid they really need.

Another problem is that there may be reactive effects of such health care. For example, psychiatric hospitalization might affect one's responses on a sexual identity test. Certainly psychiatric hospitalization changes one's self-image, and how this changed self-image is reflected in one's sexual identity is uncertain—although this will be discussed in Chapter VIII. The greater the degree to which the sexual identity test used might reflect changes due to hospitalization, the less likelihood there is that abnormal test scores might be associated with psychopathology per se.

One way to circumvent this problem is to determine overall psychological health or adjustment on the basis of scores obtained on psychological tests. While this method is free of the previously discussed problems, it has problems of its own. The main one is the truth or reliability of the individuals' responses. As noted in Chapter III, such self-report inventories are susceptible to faking or untrue responses. But if we can use tests with different weaknesses and arrive at similar results, our conclusions are strengthened.

So, in a subsequent study, I tested 366 university students (LaTorre 1978). Each was administered two tests of psychological adjustment—the Neuroticism Scale of the Eysenck Personality Inventony, and the Alienation Scale of the Psychological Screening Inventory. Along with these adjustment scales, each student was administered the BSRI.

Results from this study showed that feminine females had higher neuroticism scores than did masculine or androgynous females. Feminine males also ranked higher in neuroticism than did masculine or androgynous males. And androgynous males obtained lower alienation scores than did feminine or undifferentiated males.

The results are slightly different from the results in the 1977 study by LaTorre and Gregoire. Part of this difference may well lie in the fact that two definitions of androgyny were used. In the earlier study, the androgynous group included persons now known as undifferentiated as well as truly androgynous individuals. In the later study, the androgynous and the undifferentiated formed separate groups.

The findings were especially significant for males, in whom a feminine orientation was statistically associated with higher neuroticism scores as well as very high alienation scores. Alienation as defined by this scale is roughly equivalent to neuroticism, psychoticism, or both of a nature severe enough to warrant hospitalization.

The findings support the notion that, for the male at least, psychopathology shows itself in individuals who claim to possess a large opposite-sex aspect to their self-image. It appears that males and females defined as psychopathological represent two distinct groups with regard to sexual identity problems. In contrast to males, the females with appropriate sexual identity obtain higher psychopathology scores than those with less appropriate identity.

There could be several reasons for the finding that femininity, whether in a male or a female, is a pathological indicator. One is that femininity as a behavioral complex includes more self-disclosure than does masculinity. That is, females disclose more about themselves and are more willing to admit to certain things usually indicative of psychopathology. Hence, a person with a high femininity score would be expected to disclose more of such information. Since the measures of psychological adjustment that were used depended on self-admission of pathological indicators, it is possible that feminine individuals attained less-adjusted scores not so much because they were less adjusted as because they admitted to being less adjusted.

A similar problem has arisen in the case of transsexuals. If transsexual males are plotted on the female scale for their raw scores on the MMPI (another self-report inventory) their profile is much more normal than it is when plotted on the male scale. This would actually hold true for any male. However, since the transsexual male has a feminine sexual identity, which should include greater self-disclosure, it has been legitimately argued that he should be plotted on the female scale to correct for this fact.

However, the results I obtained are so striking that they would remain true even if the feminine males were given the benefit of having their scores compared with standardized female scores. However, such a correction factor on the female data might have erased the significance obtained.

The correlation between femininity and neuroticism could also be related to the fact that our sample was composed of college students. As shall be discussed in Chapter VII, college is basically a masculine environment. There is competition against fellow students for the top rankings that assure one of an A or a B. Oftentimes grades can be raised if the student is assertive (masculine) enough to see his teacher and cogently argue for a higher grade. In essence, the argument leads to the following conclusion: Success in college or university might very well be associated, not only with academic ability, but also with a masculine behavior pattern or masculine gender role adoption.

Individuals with a feminine sexual identity (irrespective of their biological sex) might therefore have more academic problems. Such problems actually prompt many to seek help from various sources—even psychiatry. Apparently, it is more relieving to say something is wrong with one's emotions than to admit to a lack of ability. Further, in many if not all colleges and universities, students with certified medical problems can obtain such special considerations as exemptions from examinations or extensions for submission dates of papers. And it is apparently easier to fake anxiety or psychological distress than to fake physical ailments. Hence, feminine individuals may be doing poorly at school, and some of these may then seek out psychiatric help, not because they want or need it, but because it makes them eligible for medical excuse slips. Having worked at a student health service, I know that a few students seeking psychiatric help are only interested in an excuse slip.

And the third reasons why feminine individuals could have more pathological scores is simply that femininity is associated with greater pathology. At least to a male, this seems relatively clear.

This fact is also supported when adult nonstudents are tested. Again using institutionalization to define psychological maladjustment, LaTorre, Endman, and Gossmann (1976) administered the BSRI to two groups of psychiatric patients (schizophrenic and nonschizophrenic) and a group of normal controls. Among males, both psychiatric groups tended to be androgynous; the scores for the normal males were appropriately sex typed. All three groups of females were appropriately sex typed, but the two female psychiatric groups obtained slightly more feminine scores than did the normal females. Hence we have fairly consistent evidence that, the greater the amount of femininity, the greater the chance of psychological maladjustment. However, this is most clearly and consistently shown for males. The data for females is less striking.

Theories and dozens of research studies have linked problems in sexual identity with psychoses, neruoses, and personality disorders—in fact, to virtually all psychiatric problems except those that have an organic (physical) cause or that are transient (not lasting and usually caused by a specific event such as the death of a spouse).

The Pathogenic Family

Probably the one explanation that unites these psychiatric problems in terms of etiology (origin or causation) is the role of the family. It is surprising, actually, that similar family constellations are considered the etiological basis for such a large variety of psychiatric problems. And it is even more interesting that the family constellation considered pathogenic (leading to disorder) is one that would endanger the successful development of an appropriate sexual identity.

Most research on the nature of the family in psychologically maladjusted groups has zeroed in on the family of the schizophrenic. Hence, we will use this family for demonstrative purposes. In the beginning, and even somewhat today, researchers typically examined the families of *male* schizophrenics. From this subgroup, theories, hypothesis, and findings were generalized to all schizophrenics. However, as the families of female schizophrenics began to be studied, certain important differences were noted.

Lidz (1972) and his coworkers Fleck and Cornelison did a large amount of work in this area. They, probably more than any other major theorists in this area, have noted and reported differences between the families of male and female schizophrenics.

The first pattern they determined was what they termed a "skewed" family. In such a family, it is characteristic that the mother sees her son as an extension of herself: she thinks that all her feelings, wishes, needs, and so forth also exist in her son. She tries to live out her life through him. Often, it is especially because he is male, and therefore should not be denied the things she was denied as a female, that the mother chooses him and not a daughter to fulfill her own life fantasies. Because the mother sees the son as a part of herself, she is extremely watchful over him and gives him very little freedom. She is overprotective and dominant, but at the same time can be cold and rejecting. She believes that the child could not survive on his own and that she must rule his life in order to assure both his survival and the possible fulfillment of all her desires.

Meanwhile, the mother also affects the rest of the

family. She tries to make everyone want what she wants, feel what she feels, and need what she needs. The husband may be childishly dependent on his wife, perhaps even competing with the favored son for his wife's attention. On the other hand, he may give up trying to deal with his wife's peculiarities; as a result, he divorces himself emotionally or even physically from the family.

The child is made aware that his father is a less-than-ideal figure. To be acceptable to the mother, he must become something very different from the father. Also, it becomes increasingly apparent that he represents his mother's life. He carries the burden that any attempt to separate himself from his mother could destroy her. At the same time, he feels that his own destruction is imminent if he does not separate.

It is not hard to see how the skewed family could harm the sexual identity of the male. For example, in lieu of the characteristic behavior of giving the male baby what he wants when he wants it, the mother takes care of him with a "mother knows best" attitude. He gets what she wants to give when she wants to give it. In addition, the mother clings to this child, encouraging it to cling in return. Both of these maternal behaviors are much more characteristic of a mother-daughter relationship than of a mother-son relationship. Furthermore, all of this impairs the child's sense of separateness from the mother. Such separateness is essential for the child to eventually say, "I am separate physically, and I am different physically." How can he be physically different if he is not even separate? Thus, his body image development, so important as the basis for fruther sexual identity development and the cornerstone of sexual identity formation, is retarded.

Another problem that arises concerns role models. The mother is often slightly more masculine than are mothers of other families. The father, passive and withdrawn, displays few appropriate male characteristics. Hence, the child gains a distorted sense of maleness and femaleness. This distortion would not generally take the form of sex reversal, since (especially outside the home) the parents probably do display much appropriate gender role behavior. Instead, the distortion is likely to take the form of a lack of clear differentiation between the conceptions of maleness and femaleness or at least a greater than usual perceived similarity between the sexes.

Finally, in terms of gender role adoption, it should be apparent that such feminine characteristics as dependence and yielding are reinforced more than such male characteristics as assertion and aggression. However, this is tempered by the fact that the child is being pressured to act in some ways like his mother, who we have just described, acts more manly in some ways than does the father. Confusing to you? Imagine the poor child caught in the middle of all this.

On the basis of the above scenario, sexual identity difficulties should be apparent in the male schizophrenic. It would seem that gender identity would be especially impaired. Gender role adoption may or may not be, probably depending on which specifics are being examined. Gender role preference and gender role ability would also be in danger. In fact, a review of all the research in the area of sexual identity and shizophrenia has found support for these assertions (LaTorre 1976).

The second major type of schizophrenic family is termed the "schismatic" family. This family type is associated with most of the schizophrenic females. It is known as schismatic because it is split, in contrast to the skewed family, wherein all the children give in to one family member, the mother, and the father either gives in or is emotionally or physically absent. The split in schismatic families takes the form of a war between father and mothei. Each parent openly tries to devalue and undermine the other in hopes of winning the children to his or her own side. The child is pressured to swear loyalty to one of the par nts and to renounce the other. She is caught between conflicting demands and directives.

The mother is similar to that in the skewed family. However, since the child in this family is a female, the mother feels that the child will get no further than she did as a woman. Hence, while the mother remains overprotective and believes the child cannot survive without her, she is unemotional towards the daughter. She rejects any closeness and gains no satisfaction from the daughter.

The father, as should be apparent, is drastically different from the father in the skewed family. The father in the skewed family, remember, withdraws from the family and gives in to the wife. The father in the schismatic family, in contrast, remains active within the family, if for no other reason than to try to downgrade or destroy the wife. He competes against the wife for the daughter's affection. Often the father is very seductive, promising the daughter the love that the mother denies her. The father makes it clear, however, that to obtain this love she must be very different than the mother whom he rejects openly. To complicate matters, these fathers often are insecure about their own masculinity and use their daughters to reassure themselves.

Again it should be apparent how the schismatic family can endanger the sexual identity of the female offspring. The mother rejects the daughter's being a female. She probably also rejects any show of femininity. There is little cuddling and clinging. The mother keeps the daughter close, not out of love, but in order to deny the father access to her. The mother may be even more rejecting when the daughter is an infant. She can afford to be, since the infant cannot at that time move over to the father's camp. So the relationship between mother and infant daughter is probably similar to the normal mother-and-son relationship. The daughter is made to feel separate very early. This sets the stage for the feeling of "different than mommy," which is catalyzed by the father's instilling the feeling that she *must* be different from her mommy.

The role models here, too, are confusing, but probably

not as confusing as in the skewed family. The father is playing a masculine role and the mother an only slightly masculinized feminine role. The mother's femininity is, however, deficient, especially in terms of nurturance and warmth.

The area of gender role adoption is not clear-cut. One might assume that the father would reinforce certain masculine traits in his daughter, or that both parents would, in effect, fail to reinforce appropriate feminine behaviors. Usually, though, feminity is valued since the father is looking for a woman (the daughter) to bolster his masculinity.

Hence, a female schizophrenic from a schismatic family could have sexual identity problems, but the likelihood of such problems is less than for a male schizophrenic from a skewed family. And again the research evidence bears this out. Female schizophrenics do display some sexual identity problems, but the findings are neither as consistent nor as clearly established as those for male schizophrenics (LaTorre 1976).

The family of the schizophrenic has been discussed because most of the research has concentrated on it. However, the disturbed relationships just described are not specific to schizophrenia. Many kinds of psychopathology are associated with such families (Heilbrun 1968; Kinsey 1966; Zwerling 1971).

One should not become too sweeping, however, in the application of sexual identity problems to psychopathology. Certainly it would be pretentious to suggest that sexual identity problems in and of themselves cause psychopathology. I believe a more conservative, and accurate, hypothesis would be that sexual identity problems play a major role among all the sources of anxiety that may compound to increase the likelihood of a maladaptive response to the environment.

In essence, this hypothesis suggests that each individual has some breaking point, which in psychological terminology is known as the individual's *vulnerability*. Anxiety, pressures, conflicts and problems all bring the individual closer to his breaking point, or increase *risk*. The greater the vulnerability, the greater is the risk posed by any problem. In this framework, sexual identity problems are seen as a major source of all those things that increase an individual's risk. It seems fairly certain that, with some pathologies, including schizophrenia, a high degree of vulnerability is inherited.

Therefore, the fact that sexual identity problems exist does not necessarily mean that psychopathology will develop. It depends on the individual's vulnerability. An individual with a low inherited vulnerability may sustain many problems including sexual identity confusion. On the other hand, a person without sexual identity problems may show psychopathological symptoms if he is highly vulnerable or has had a number of other problems that increased his risk.

However, the consistent finding of sexual identity problems in psychopathological groups, makes these problems especially significant among risk factors in leading to psychopathology. It is probable that the lack of a clearly established sexual identity leaves one with a deep confusion regarding his basic self-identity and a feeling that the very self is in jeopardy. This sets in motion a process whereby the individual digs himself more deeply into a state of confusion and alienation, with a subsequent inability to deal with risk factors. The process results eventually in a pathological mode of functioning.

Obviously, then, the establishment of a clear and secure gender identity helps greatly in the individual's eventual development. Parents can help "immunize" their children against such problems in self-identity by monitoring their own reactions and behavior toward their offspring. By helping the child to develop along appropriate sex lines and by encouraging body-image definitions, parents can greatly benefit the child's subsequent psychological adjustment.

In the area of gender role, parents should first provide good and appropriate models of gender role

behavior, and second should reinforce behavior appropriate for their child's sex. This should be a natural
process, not forced. In essence, it should not be overdone
but simply should be done. This is normally a subtle
process, and, should a person be unable to do this naturally, perhaps he himself should seek professional help.

The developing child has enough confusions in his
life. Gender role differences should not be one of them.
The establishment of an appropriate sexual identity is essential to the development of a mature and healthy
personality.

Summary

The relationship between sexual identity and psychopathology is well noted. It has theoretical roots in the
works of von Krafft-Ebing, Freud, and Adler. Dozens of
research studies have empirically supported these theories. Psychoses, neuroses, and personality disturbances
have all been linked to problems in sexual identification.
It is proposed that the family is the main force for either
helping the child develop an appropriate identity or for
undermining the child's identity. Individuals with psychological problems generally had parents who were not
good role models and/or did not provide the right pattern
of reinforcement. Still, sexual identity problems alone
probably do not cause psychopathology. But certainly
the lack of a clear sexual identity is a major source of risk
that interacts with the individual's state of vulnerability.
Sexual identity is a basic building block in the establishment of a mature and healthy personality.

V.
Sexual Variations and Sexual Identity

In this chapter, I shall explore the relationships between sexual identity and sexual variations. *Sexual variation* is a term that is gaining widespread acceptance and replaces such terms as *sexual deviation* and *sexual perversion*. The new term is more acceptable since the word *variation* implies less abnormality or less moral censure than do the words *deviation* and *perversion*. The change reflects the increasing cultural acceptance of behaviors that occur between consenting adults.

Transsexuality

The first group of individuals I should like to discuss is the transsexuals. As explained earlier, these individuals have a self-concept of being the sex opposite to their biological sex. That is, they have a gender identity reversal. This reversal prompts them to adopt and prefer the opposite gender role. Many transsexuals are so sure

71

of a gender identity contradictory to their biological sex that they seek out and obtain surgery to make their body image correspond to their gender identity.

Obviously, physicians do not provide sex changes to just anyone who wants them. The usual prerequisites include both a thorough screening process and at least a one-year period of living as a member of the opposite sex. Ideally, sex-change surgery is provided if the person meets the following criteria: (1) a lifelong sense or feeling of being a member of the opposite sex; (2) early and persistent cross-dressing coupled with a lack of erotic feelings associated with cross-dressing; and (3) a disdain or repugnance for homosexual behavior. When gender identity clinics first opened, they were surprised at how many classic cases of transsexuality they received. Everyone who came in had the same story: "I want a sex change operation. I've always felt I was a girl (or boy). Since I was three years old, I've cross-dressed, but it doesn't turn me on. And I get absolutely no satisfaction from my penis [vagina and clitoris]."

However, it soon became apparent that word had spread throughout the transsexual community on what one had to say if one wanted to obtain the sex-change surgery. And it also became disappointingly apparent that such textbook cases did not exist. Fisk (1973) has argued that each primary diagnosis of gender dysphoria syndrome (another name for transsexualism) should be accompanied by diagnoses such as: (1) effeminate homosexuality, (2) transvestism, (3) inadequate schizoid personality, (4) recovered or residual psychosis, or (5) exhibitionistic sociopathy (a term covering those who want a sex change in order to become rich and famous). Hence, the transsexual requesting sex change surgery is not a simple phenomenon. And it is important for the clinician to exclude from the program individuals who are the furthest away from ideal transsexualism.

Transsexuals are, by definition, individuals whose sexual identity is incongruent with their biological sex.

They are therefore appropriate for inclusion in this chapter. In addition, they rank as a major resource for individuals examining sexual identity in all its aspects. Because transsexuals are known to have sexual identity reversals, there is no need to discuss proof of this. What will be discussed is a possible cause of this phenomenon.

A large body of research has dealt with possible biological antecedents to transsexualism. In almost every psychological problem area, a biological cause is sought. The reason is twofold. First, a biological problem is generally more amenable to a well-defined cure than is a psychological problem. Second, a biological explanation relieves the individual from any feelings of guilt or shame. After all, he cannot control his biology.

While studies demonstrate that one can *biologically* masculinize a female or feminize a male, there is no conclusive evidence that transsexualism—*psychological* masculinization of a female or feminization of a male— has biological underpinnings. In a few exceptional cases, biological abnormalities that could affect masculinity or femininity have been noted (e.g. lowered testicular androgen due to pituitary deficiency or presence of an XXY sex-chromosome pattern). Yet the evidence on most transsexuals fails to show any biological difference between them and nontranssexuals.

Hence, while paying lip service to possible biological antecedents and not completely ruling them out, most researchers have attempted to determine a psychological explanation for transsexualism. The one most adopted includes, again, the family as a predisposing agent. Descriptions of such families presented in this chapter derive mainly from the work of Green (1974), who has done much work with transsexuals and has a long-term program underway for feminine boys, and from Stoller (1972), who seems to be one of the few researchers interested in the etiology of female transsexualism.

Interestingly, the families of transsexuals share many characteristics with the families of schizophrenics and other psychopathological groups. In the families of male transsexuals, for example, there is a symbiotic relationship between the mother and the son. The mother creates and sustains this throughout the earliest years of the child's life. This excessive maternal attention, and the resulting increase in physical contact, impedes the child's sense of separation from the mother; so his basic body image does not readily form.

Maternal dominance is not checked by the father, who is powerless or even absent. So even the role models available to the child are less than adequate.

But the real problem seems to center on reinforcement of the child's gender role adoption. Many psychopathological families either reinforce inappropriate gender role behavior or fail to reinforce appropriate gender role adoption, but the male transsexual's family goes to extremes in this matter. It actively undermines the boy's gender role adoption. In the first years of life, the mother actually encourages feminine behavior in her son. In many cases, the mother wants a daughter so badly that she sees the son as a little girl—denying the boy's biological sex. Even more often, one finds that any feminine behavior in the son is treated with indifference—a subtle encouragement—while any masculine behavior is punished. This is especially true of rough-and-tumble play, which is prohibited by the overly protective mother.

In school, the child gravitates towards female playmates, rejecting both male peers and male toys and games. This behavior is disapproved of by his peers, and the resulting anxiety is alleviated only by retreating back home to mommy, who openly allows his feminine characteristics.

Many teachers, of course, enjoy the shy, well-mannered, quiet, and obedient male child. He makes their work easier. They reinforce this behavior pattern and the child may become the teacher's pet. This leads to further ostracism by the boys in his class but serves to alleviate some of the anxiety which has, until now, only been relieved by mommy.

The mother is actually thrilled by her son's femininity. She helped produce and encourage it. The mother conspires with her son, allowing him to openly express his feminine qualities at home. The father is much less significant in this child's life. In fact, most male transsexuals note their preference for, and greater closeness with, the mother. The father lets the mother have her way with the boy when he is tiny. As the son grows older, the father may become interested in father-son activities, but by that time the son is so much of a mamma's boy that he refuses to participate. This rejection of manly activities further alienates the father, and a snowball effect is in progress.

This family pattern is similar to the psychopathological family pattern and differs only in the more open acceptance and encouragement of femininity.

The family of the female transsexual has been studied less than the family of the male transsexual. One reason is that the transsexual population is chiefly male. Estimates of the ratio of male to female transsexuals range from two to one to almost nine to one. This supports a consistent finding: Sexual identity is more problematic, harder to develop, and more susceptible to developmental errors for the male than it is for the female.

An interesting pattern has been proposed for the female transsexual. From the beginning, the parents see the child as a less than perfect female (which could be said of any baby girl). The mother-daughter relationship is atypical. The mother does not cuddle the daughter but lets her alone to be on her own. This gives the child an unusually great sense of separateness from the mother. Many of the mothers claim it is the child who does the pushing away; perhaps these mothers are projecting the masculinity they wish to see in the daughter.

The mother is affectively removed from the daugher and is often preoccupied with emotional problems of her own. The father rejects the mother and her problems, divorcing himself emotionally. The daughter not only has poor or almost nonexistent role models but is encouraged to "take the father's place." This alleviates the father's guilt about not fulfilling his responsibility to his wife, and it helps the mother by giving her someone to lean on.

The father, although distant from the mother, is warm and friendly with the daughter who is doing him a great service. However, instead of treating her like a female, he shares his masculine interests with her. She develops a closeness with him that she should have had with the mother. The daughter adores the father but despises the mother, her problems, and even her femaleness, which could be seen as her weakness. The girl develops masculine characteristics because (1) she learns to value them more than femininity, (2) she is forced to in her role as a "husband substitute" for her mother, and (3) masculinity is reinforced by both the father and the mother. The masculine skills fostered by the family coalesce into a masculine identity.

So again we see the effects of parents not displaying appropriate gender role behavior themselves and not reinforcing it in their children. And, in this case, we see the effects of reinforcing opposite-gender role behavior.

Homosexuality

The next sexual variation to be discussed is homosexuality. As mentioned previously, it is often difficult to differentiate between effeminate homosexuality and transsexualism. Strictly speaking, the homosexual is defined in behavioral terms, as one who has sexual relations with members of his own biological sex. By definition, his gender identity is secure and congruent with his biological sex. If it is not, then the term transsexual should be considered. While it would be ideal to have clear-cut boundaries between homosexuals and transsexuals, such is not always the case in real life. For example, there is one self-admitted "transsexual male" in St. Louis, Missouri, who underwent sex-change surgery and now, as a "female," engages in sexual relations only with females. This transsexual defines herself as a "homosexual female."

Also, the behavioral definition of a homosexual as one who actually engages in sexual relations with members of his own biological sex precludes direct comparison with heterosexuals because a person can be labeled heterosexual without ever engaging in sexual relations with members of the opposite sex. Heterosexuality is actually defined as lack of homosexuality. No matter how many homosexual fantasies or desires a person has, until he consummates them he is not considered homosexual. Yet a person could lead a life of abstinence and still be classified as heterosexual.

Despite these problems, for the purpose of this discussion the term *homosexual* will refer to those who prefer and have sexual relations with members of their own biological sex. This type of individual was the subject of most of the studies of homosexuality that form the basis of the following discussion.

As mentioned in Chapter 3, it was originally believed that homosexuals had a sexual identity reversal. They often served as the validation group for tests of sexual identity. However, with the exception of the specific "sexual relations with one's own biological sex," there is little consistent evidence that homosexuals, as a whole, demonstrate sexual identity reversal. The early confusion sprang partly from the fact that the homosexuals studied at the beginning of the century were psychiatric patients. At that time, our culture was not open to the gay community, and therefore homosexuals were not as willing to admit to their sexual preference as they are today. Only the case histories of those few who sought psychiatric help and disclosed their homosexuality to their therapist were taken into consideration. Since psychopathology per se is associated with sexual identity dysfunction, it is not surprising that homosexuals were declared to have sexual identity problems.

More recent work with nonpatient homosexuals seems to have tempered this belief. First, homosexuality is no more a unitary phenomenon than is trans-sexualism or schizophrenia. Even years ago, people realized that there were many varieties of homosexuality and attempted to subcategorize the phenomenon with such labels as passive homosexual, active homosexual, insertor, insertee, latent homosexual, genuine homosexual, pseudohomosexual, and sexual invert. While this was a valid effort, there seemed to be more cases that did not fit the categories than that did. For example, it appears that the male homosexual who penetrates also is penetrated. Apparently, most male homosexuals need ejaculation for gratification, and the partner wants to be satisfied, too.

The wide variety in the homosexual subculture helps us see the wide range of sexual identity variation. There are a few homosexuals who are dissatisfied with their biological sex and wish they had been born as the opposite sex but are unwilling to change their gender as adults. There are male homosexuals who dress and act like males, and there are those who dress in drag and adopt feminine mannerisms. This role mimickry is becoming less and less apparent as homosexuality is gaining wider acceptance. As a result, several investigators have reasoned that role mimickry is an attempt to justify a preference for same-sex individuals. In essence, the individual is believed to think, "It's okay to have sex with another man because I act and dress like a woman." This theory would also indicate that role-mimicking individuals are less accepting of their homosexuality than are homosexuals who appear masculine. Due to such insecurity, it is no wonder that mimickers might seek out prefessional help to deal with their problems.

Even regarding the sexual identity specific most relevant to this group, sexual relations with same-sex individuals, there is considerable variation. Many are exclusive homosexuals, but some do enjoy opposite-sex partners, too. In an attempt to delineate these latter individuals, the term bisexual was introduced.

On sexual identity tests that differentiate transsexuals at one pole and nontranssexual heterosexuals at the other pole, a heterogeneous group of homosexuals may score at either pole or between the poles. They comprise, indeed, a conglomerate of individuals with a complete range of sexual identity. The only thing they have in common is the sexual identity specific of same-sex partners. Interestingly, despite the wide variation in behavior, male homosexuals tend to retain the male pattern of having sexual relations with a large number of partners and having sex for its own sake. Even male transsexuals tend to follow this pattern. Female homosexuals retain the female pattern of having sex with a limited number of partners and keeping it within the context of an emotional relationship.

Researchers and homosexuals alike would of course be happy to demonstrate a biological cause for homosexuality. But both have been disappointed. Biology seems to underly how much sex one tries to have, but it is uncorrelated with what type of partner one has sexual relations with.

After reviewing studies concerned with the causative factors in homosexuality, Thompson and McCandless (1976) decided that the family, again, was the culprit. Once more, we find different family constellations depending on whether the homosexual offspring is male or female. And, once again, there are disturbing similarities between these family types and the family types of psychopathological groups and groups of transsexuals.

The mother of the homosexual is described as having an intense, overprotective, seductive, dominating, and restrictive relationship with her son. Mother and son are exceptionally close both physically and emotionally, which probably impedes the sense of separateness the boy needs to evolve a male body image.

In terms of gender role adoption, it appears that the key figure is the father. The most clear-cut picture of the mother is that she is dominant in the family. The father, however, has been variously described as detached, absent (physically or emotionally), hostile or critical, and ineffective. Such traits lead to a disturbed relationship between father and son. In some cases, the father even overtly expresses his dislike or hatred for his son. In return, the developing homosexual male spends little time with his father, fears him, realizes that his father does not like him, and probably does not accept or respect his father.

In this case, the father almost actively drives the son away. The boy therefore turns to his mother, who is all too ready and willing to take him under her wing. The child places a negative value on his father and even on maleness. The mother is positively valued, as are her female traits such as warmth and interdependence.

Less is known about female homosexuals—possibly because there are fewer female than male homosexuals, or possibly because male homosexuality is perceived as a greater problem to society than female homosexuality. However, the following seems to be a typical family constellation.

The mother of the female homosexual tends to be overburdened or ill-equipped for mothering. She often sees herself as persecuted. Perhaps because of her preoccupation with herself, she has little time to interact with her child. So we can suspect a forced separateness. The only closeness the mother gives the child is for selfish reasons. The mother either needs attention from the child because she is not receiving any from her husband, or else she wants an ally against the father. Therefore, there seems to be some split in the family of the female homosexual.

The father's role seems especially important. Homosexual females report more mutual relationships with their fathers than with their mothers. The father is dominated by the mother and ineffectively seeks to obtain his daughter's love. He becomes possessive and even seductive. He rejects her development as a mature female, for when she matures she will start to date other men and be lost to the father. The mother also interferes with the girl's heterosexual development, possibly because the older woman has found so little pleasure in such relationships that she tries to prevent the younger from enjoying them. The mother often even encourages masculine behavior.

The three presentations of family types in the last two chapters have outlined how the family can undermine the sexual identity of the child. The similarities among these family types are amazing. In fact, one might wonder how different behavioral patterns can arise from such similar backgrounds. Fortunately, there are enough differences to offer a possible explanation. For example, the family of the male transsexual is especially open in encouraging the child's femininity. The parents of the female homosexual discourage heterosexuality much more than do the parents of the other families. Subtle but important differences such as these must be extracted in order to explain the different courses that sexual identity problems can take. Not enough attention has yet been paid to family differences *among* such important groups. To date, most of the effort has been directed toward determining differences between any one of these groups and the families of normal groups. So gross variations from the norm (which are similar among all of our special groups) are noted, but smaller differences are glossed over.

The remainder of this chapter will deal with several other types of sexual variance. Special reference will be given to the role that sexual identity plays for them. Families will not be discussed in detail because few studies have been done on the family backgrounds of these individuals.

Transvestism

The next sexual variation to be discussed is transvestism, which occurs almost exclusively among males. Transvestism, or dressing in clothing of the opposite sex, is not the same as transsexualism or effeminate homosexuality. Transvestites cross-dress for erotic sensations. The act is a turn-on in itself. Male transvestites have a feeling and sense of being male and normally have sexual relations with females. Again, this is the textbook or ideal definition. Many intermediate categories are observed.

The family background of male transvestites includes a symbiotic but hostile mother-son relationship and a distant, passive father (Spensley and Barter 1971). The mother denigrates the son's striving for masculinity and in many cases even encourages his cross-dressing behavior.

Even though male transvestites by definition have male gender identity and gender role adoption (except for the cross-dressing specific), it would seem that the transvestite could be very confused about his sexual identity. The cross-dressing may serve to let him try out both possible body images. Unlike the transsexuaal, who is sure of his sex-reversed gender identity, the transvestite is unsure.

This conflict may become extremely acute: many an adolescent has committed suicide while cross-dressed (Bakwin and Bakwin 1966). Even a leading professional in the field, a self-proclaimed transvestite who once argued that transvestites had no sexual identity problems, has appeared in public under a female first name. Despite what transvestites would like to think of themselves, persistent cross-dressing should be taken as a sign of sexual identity problems. Occasional cross-dressing for thrills is often a part of normal development. But the behavior can reach such proportions as to be a pathological indicator and one of possibly severe consequence, at least to an adolescent.

Nymphomania and Satyriasis

Another sexual variation is sexual overindulgence: nymphomania in the female and satyriasis in the male.

One hypothesis is that these people are compelled to engage in heterosexual activity repetitively to allay a basic anxiety related to a persistent doubt about their sexual identity (Gershman 1970).

The male who boasts of a large number of conquests does so to try to prove his masculinity. "See how much of a man I am. See, the proof is in all the females I have penetrated with my penis." Further, the act of penetration itself, and the stream of female bodies he uses, serve to enhance his sense of difference from the female sex and to reinforce his own body image. Such a probable sexual identity problem as this type of male was guessed many years ago (another name given to satyriasis is the Don Juan complex). It was suggested that these people are latent homosexuals who are trying to deny their homosexual feelings by engaging in as much heterosexual behavior as possible. The main characteristic of this group is, not so much the large number of females they have coitus with, but their compulsive drive to seek out large numbers of partners. In this way the person proves to himself and others that he is indeed a man.

The nymphomaniac also has long been suspected of sexual identity problems. As with the male, the act of coitus serves to reinforce her body image. The many penetrations she receives reinforces a female image, and the large number of male bodies she sees assures her that there is a difference between her body and a male's body. Superficially, she seems to be the antithesis of the female homosexual, but actually both behaviors are probably manifestations of the same basic problem. Unlike the female homosexual, the nymphomaniac rebels against her parents' attempts to curb her heterosexuality.

Family constellations appear to be similar to the family types already discussed, albeit much less work has been done, and most of the evidence comes from case-history and self-report material.

Exhibitionism

Exhibitionists are also thought to have sexual

identity problems. Essentially, it is believed they expose themselves to prove to themselves and others that they are indeed males. This is another variation in which males have cornered the market. Perhaps any female's exhibitionistic tendencies are alleviated through such modern forms of dress as no bras, see-through blouses, and thong bikinis. In fact, one survey demonstrated that promiscuous females tend to wear more seductive clothing than other women do. Possibly promiscuity overrides exhibitionism in the female. After all, a female who exhibits her body generally has many opportunitites for sexual encounters, since many of the males to whom she exhibits herself may approach her for sexual purposes. The male exhibitionist, however, is usually ignored by his target or else scares her off. Perhaps the exhibitionist is a frustrated Don Juan.

Sadism and Masochism

These behaviors represent exaggerated forms of masculinity and femininity, respectively. Perhaps, by overdoing it, sadists and masochists attain more of a sense of their sexual identity. It is not surprising, then, that sadists are typically males and masochists are typically females. However—and this is where we have some indication of the sexual identity conflict in these individuals—sadists often display some masochistic qualities, and masochists are occasionally sadistic. Sadism and masochism are often seen together in the same person. Hence, the person is struggling between an exaggerated masculinity and an exaggerated femininity.

Exhibitionism, sadism, and masochism are not discussed in greater detail because little is known of their causation or the families from which they spring. Possibly because they are less common than such variations as homosexuality, they have been studied less. However, they have been presented to show the extensiveness and variety of sexual identity problems.

Summary

Transsexuals, most of whom are male, believe they are the opposite sex from their biological gender. They act and dress like the opposite sex and prefer to have sexual relations with members of their own biological sex. Homosexuals also have sexual relations with their own sex. However, these people differ considerably in the maleness or femaleness of their dress and actions. Transvestites obtain erotic excitement by wearing clothes of the opposite sex. They seldom have sexual relations with their own sex and usually act like their biological sex. These three groups have, in a sense, given in to a sexual identity problem. However, other sexual variations are an attempt to deny such a problem. For example, exhibitionists expose themselves in order to reassure themselves and others that they are, indeed, men. Nymphomaniacs and satyrs are those who attempt to reassure themselves and others of their sexual identity by overdoing sexual relations and thereby "proving" that they are real men or real women. Although the family backgrounds of some of these variants are not well documented, the data indicate that all spring from similar, distorted family backgrounds. Psychopathological groups also have the same general kinds of families. What is needed is less attention to differences between these families and normal families, and more study of family differences among these groups.

VI.

The Feminized Classroom

Until now, I have emphasized the effect of the family on the child's emerging sexual identity. And the family not only plays the most significant role in the all-important development of gender identity, but also is the first agent to affect the child's gender role. However gender role is somewhat amenable to change, and later socialization experiences can affect it.

The second-most-significant socializing agent is the school or preschool. Here, the child has a mother substitute and a number of unchosen peers with whom to interact. As should be apparent from the title of this chapter, I agree with Biller (1973) that elementary school has a tendency to feminize children. Much of what I shall discuss actually comes from Biller's thesis.

In order to highlight this belief that elementary school has a feminizing effect, let me give a personalized account of a school day. All of us have gone through some

elementary grades and will probably find parts of this
story familiar. However, I shall be discussing such a day
from a teacher's perspective, for one day I acted as
substitute teacher for a second-grade class.

First I note a conspicuous overrepresentation of
female teachers. The vice-principal is also a female, but
the principal is a male.

When the bell rings, the children are supposed to
have neatly arranged their winter coats and boots in
their lockers and have seated themselves quietly at their
respective desks. Any monkey business is met with a
disapproving look. A few pleasantries are exchanged,
and a few of the boys raise their voices over the other
children's.

I ask the children what normally happens in the
mornings and meet with more raised voices (boys), gig-
gling, and movement in the seats (again boys). The class
threatens to get out of hand so I reprimand them—gently.
After all, this is my first day and I need not contend
with this permanently.

Finally, reading is chosen, and I spend over an hour
with two different reading groups. The first group has the
more advanced readers. They take turns going to the
front of the classroom and acting like teacher by calling
on other children to read. The little boys, again, make the
most strenuous attempts to be recognized. They lie across
their desks, half standing and raise their hands as high
as they can, calling, "Me! Me! Me!" When girls act as
teacher, they hesitate and are not sure whom to call, but
they appear to take their teacher role seriously. The boys
take the situation more as a game, and it is necessary to
relieve at least one from his appointed teacher's post.
Incidentally, the girls are better readers.

While the advanced group reads, the slower group
(consisting of three boys) is expected to do some writing
exercises geared toward helping them with vocabulary
and reading skills. However, one of these boys sits and
draws instead. Even after several verbal inquiries and

directives, he still does not obey or yield. So I stand right over him and help him, step by step, do what he is supposed to do.

Then, when I take the slower group for reading, the other group has written exercises. This is a most exasperating experience. Students constantly ask what to do, wonder how many times to write the sentences, and complain that they have run out of paper. The boys are noticeably unable to silently sit and do the exercises. They talk, throw things to one another, move about, ask silly questions, or sharpen their pencils—which are already sharper than a great white shark's tooth. Finally, I am pushed past my limit by two boys carrying on a verbal and nonverbal interaction. In an attempt to hide it from me, one of them has stood his book up on his desk. I approach him slowly from behind, looking at the other side of the room so as not to give any clues to my intentions, and then kick the book off his desk! "Pick it up and knock off the noise in here!" I boom in a roaring voice. The child blushes and nervously and sheepishly picks up the book. The class falls silent. Naturally, the silence does not last the rest of the day, but nonetheless I have dominated for a time.

At recess I am asked to supervise the girls' yard (yes, boys and girls are separated). I feel a strange revulsion as the girls start to hang around me, getting closer and closer, and eventually shoot out their hands for fleeting grasps of mine, which grasps become longer and longer. This is certainly not my idea of a recess. People are supposed to run and shout. So I commandeer a ball and a quick game of kickball begins. Still, many girls are more interested in chasing me than in chasing the ball.

After such a frustrating recess, I decide to carry on indoors. So we play "Army." One student is designated battalion commander, and four students serve as company commanders. The rest are members of the companies. The command positions are rotated. The boys come through with glorious colors and resound commands to the troops. But I just cannot find a loud-mouthed girl. Even the most active girl in the class fails to yell out commands, despite constant prodding and help.

After lunch, I request to have gym with the children. I am told that I am lucky. They only have gym once a week, but they have not had it yet that week. Furthermore, the regular teacher does not like gym; so she will be happy that I have taken the gym period for the week. Again the boys can show their stuff. What they lack in schoolroom discipline and academic prowess, they make up for in physical strength and stamina. In fact, even in gym it is necessary to reprimand the boys. Apparently they do not like to follow rules or stay within certain limits.

Most of the rest of the day is spent in paper, pencil, and crayon activities. This serves as a time-out for me. A few songs and some cheers are also included. And, at the end of the day, a little boy is segregated for pushing and shoving in line.

This account illustrates two phenomena. First little boys and little girls show different behavioral patterns. Little girls are relatively passive, obedient, neat, and attentive, and they enjoy different types of activities than do boys, who are more restless, active, aggressive, and impulsive. This is not an isolated observation. In fact, studies have shown that even three-year-olds have adopted gender role behaviors. In preschools, boys and girls that age differ in their play activities. Boys usually like blocks, transportation toys, and the sandbox. Girls usually engage in art work, play with dolls, and play house. The average child enters the school environment already behaving in line with his appropriate gender role.

The second phenomenon that should be noted is the socializing agent's behavior. In the second-grade class described above, I was the socializing agent, the teacher. Note how my attempt at socialization tended to reinforce a feminine behavioral pattern. However, being a male, I also attempted to have students act in some masculine ways, such as playing kickball and giving commands. Boys especially took the brunt of the feminine socialization, because they acted in masculine ways that were disruptive to the class. Girls already acted femininely. They sat in their seats quietly and obeyed my every directive. It was unnecessary to socialize them.

The Female Teacher

This feminization is even more striking with a female teacher. It has been noted that women teachers tend to reinforce feminine behaviors irrespective of the sex of the child. Fagot and Patterson (1969) observed four female preschool teachers and noted incidents in which the teachers reinforced various sex-typed behaviors. Behaviors that were not sex-typed were excluded from study. Of 233 incidents in which the teachers reinforced boys' behavior, 199, or approximately 86%, followed the boys' involvements in feminine behaviors! Only 14% of the reinforcements followed masculine behavior. Of 363 incidents in which the teachers reinforced girls' behaviors, 353, or 97%, involved feminine behaviors. Masculine behaviors by girls were reinforced only 3% of the time. Therefore it is quite apparent that feminine teachers reinforce femininity irrespective of the sex of the child.

Boys enter school with an intense motivation to behave like a man. Still, most of them are relatively insecure in their role status. This insecurity is compounded by the presence of female authority figures and by the female teachers' reinforcement of feminine behavior. The emphasis on conformity, obedience, neatness, and passivity is antithetical to the roles boys have been expected to play. Even the female first graders pose a threat to the six-year-old male's self-image of dominance and competence: girls at that age have greater developmental maturity than boys do.

It has been further suggested that female teachers pick on their male students. There is proof that female teachers give girls better grades even when boys have objectively achieved a higher level of performance (Hanson 1959). Boys also receive more negative reactions and less reinforcement than do girls in elementary school.

Another area that can cause a split between boys and female teachers is athletics. Boys are interested in playing rough-and-tumble games, ready to clobber a ball (or another child), and eager to demonstrate their physical abilities. Female teachers, however, often withdraw from this area. As shown in the personal account of a school day, recess for girls and female teachers must consist mainly of walking and talking in the schoolyard. Many female teachers do not like gym period and certainly rate it as one of the lesser necessary classes, even though it already occurs much less often than do academic classes. Actually, this downplay of gym not only sets up a schism between the male children and the female teacher, but it deprives the boys of a constructive outlet for pent-up frustration and aggression. Without this appropriate outlet the children become more prone to act out their aggressive tendencies and their restlessness in the classroom itself. This produces what teachers call a "behavorial problem." It is no coincidence that the majority of behavioral problems are boys. And rowdy behavior further alienates the female teacher from the male student.

In fact, it has been indicated that the boys who do manage to do well in elementary school are the more feminine boys—those who are obedient, neat, and yielding. The more masculine boys fare poorly.

Probably a number of female readers are becoming upset with my constant reference to femininity as passive, obedient, and neat. This is not meant in a disparaging way. These qualities can be desirable, and in elementary school they are certainly necessary. There is nothing wrong with neatness or obedience. In fact, they are actually more desirable than unkemptness and disobedience. These references are meant to reflect the gender role adoption that anyone can observe. In elementary school more girls than boys are neat and obedient. The two sexes are socialized and reinforced to behave the way they do, and the basis of the differential reinforcement and socialization is biological sex.

An additional problem a boy faces is in terms of modeled behavior. The elementary school girl has an appropriate and constant model of femininity—the female teacher. Certainly the boy sees the teacher as a positively valued being and would like to emulate her qualities. But if all his preschool and elementary school teachers are women, his role models are very limited. The behaviors he would emulate tend to be feminine.

The only male authority in the elementary school may be the principal or vice-principal. And, unfortunately, the only child who sees this man is the already too-masculine boy. He is the classroom disturber, the nonconformist, the disobedient child. And he is sent to the office to receive fatherlike punishment. The more feminine boy who is doing well in school and is not a behavior problem has little interaction with the male disciplinarian. And it is precisely this child who most needs interaction with adult males. Certainly he will do well in elementary school but his sexual identity may be so disturbed that he will not make it in such masculine areas of life as job hunting and university achievement.

Peers and Parents

One wonders, then, with all this feminine influence, how a male child survives elementary school still wearing pants, enjoying football, being a daredevil, and scorning authority. The answer apparently lies in interaction with peers and, of course, with the family, which remains a major force and socializing agent.

The same study (Fagot and Patterson) that demonstrated teacher reinforcement of feminine behavior also assessed peer reinforcement. It was found that less than 1% of all reinforcement given by peers was for opposite-sex behavior. That is, almost all reinforcement that a young child gives to another child occurs when the other child does something in line with his appropriate gender role, or at least is neutral with regard to gender role. It was also found that boys reinforce other boys more often than they reinforce girls and that girls reinforce girls more often than they reinforce boys.

So it seems that male peers are the main salvation of the elementary school male's masculine style of behavior. (Remember the two boys carrying on a verbal and non-verbal interaction and hiding behind the book?) Still, the teacher and school must have some effect and, therefore, it is not surprising that male children have more learning disability, more reading problems, more behavioral problems, lower grades, and less interest in school than do female children.

A crucial role is also played by the father, a major source of masculine reinforcement for the young boy. Should the boy feel rejected by the father, he may seek reinforcement from the mother or teacher, both of whom tend to bring out the child's femininity. The child will become more feminine in order to obtain the reinforcement he so desperately desires.

The feminized classroom, while exerting a slightly deleterious effect on all male children, is even more hazardous for the male child who enters elementary school with sexual identity confusion. If a boy's father is physically or emotionally absent, openly rejects his son, or presents a poor gender role model, the child is at a decided disadvantage in his attempt to resolve his sexual identity. The school mercilessly pounds its feminizing requirements into this child.

Such children can become so preoccupied with their familial problems that they cannot deal adequately with their academia. They may also need so much attention that their efforts to gain this attention are misdirected from acceptable attention (attaining high grades) to unacceptable attention (punching other students or stealing).

On the other hand, many of these children, raised already in a feminine environment, find the feminized classroom a pleasure. They succeed in school and become favorites of the teacher. Their peers, however, may very well shun them. At the same time that these boys become academically adept at the elementary level, they set the stage for personal problems in later life.

The Male Teacher

This feminized classroom thesis is not being overdone. As further proof, studies have been conducted on classroom differences that depend on the teacher's biological sex. It has been demonstrated, for example, that male elementary school teachers are more objective than female teachers and give fairer grades, whereas women give girls better grades even though they may not deserve them (Arnold 1968). In addition, there is less of a schism between male teacher and male pupil, and more masculine behavior is accepted. As a result, boys do better in school with male teachers than with female teachers.

And the evidence shows no deleterious effects on the female child. This could be for one of three reasons. First, the male teacher may be more permissive, child-centered, and flexible than the female teacher. When I taught, I was chided by some of the women teachers for letting the student go beyond some basic (to them) limits. Second, the male teacher's masculinity might be tempered by the school's femininity. Even I had to reinforce certain limits and encourage obedience in order to prevent chaos. Third, elementary teaching is largely a feminine occupation, as determined by the female to male ratio of teachers, and the men in the profession may use certain of their feminine qualities along with their masculine qualities.

In fact, the presence of male teachers seems to alleviate many of the problems that harass young boys. In cultures where most elementary school teachers are male, boys do not have more reading problems than girls, as is true in our society. Instead, boys and girls read about equally well. And the presence of a male teacher seems to aid both male and female pupils in developing spatial and analytic abilties.

Textbooks

Another important socializing agent is the child's academic material. Thumb through some of the elementary school readers. Jack and John and their father go on a rough boat ride. Jill and Sue and their mother cook the meal and wash the dishes. John chases the dog, Spot, but Jill becomes upset when Spot jumps up on her new dress. Other male figures in these stories are policemen, firemen, doctors, forest rangers, airline pilots, sailors, farmers and astronauts. Female figures are nurses, stewardesses, or teachers. Many major textbook publishers now have guidelines prohibiting this approach, but which textbooks are adopted is usually the prerogative of older, traditional-gender-role socialized parents and teachers.

History books praise Florence Nightingale because of her nursing abilities (nurturance, warmth, soothing others' miseries) and glorify Hannibal for his masculine efforts (crossing the Alps with elephants, aggression, dominance). Science books show the boy holding the test tubes and the girl looking on with her arms by her sides.

These elementary school books provide an essential source of socialization, which is probably more important for the boy than for the girl. Despite the female teacher's unconscious efforts to socialize him femininely, the boy has picture proof of what types of things he should become in life. Peers and adult male figures support these images, which could be the reason that boys more than girls are elementary school casualities. The most vulnerable child is the male who enters school with a confused sexual identity. Such confusion combined with peer rein-forcement of male behavior and teacher reinforcement of female behavior must produce quite an anxiety-pro-voking conflict.

Peers, the father, and school books tend to give the male child some more-appropriate perspective on gender role divisions. Male teachers help considerably and, in fact, seem also to be of benefit to female pupils.

Summary

It has long been noted that male children have more trouble in school than do female children. That is, more boys in the elementary grades have learning disabilities and behavior problems than do girls. Until recently, this sex difference had been attributed to the different natures of boys and girls. However, this problem has now been linked to the feminized atmosphere of the elementary school classroom. With few exceptions, elementary school teachers are females. It has been demonstrated that female teachers reinforce female behavior irrespec-tive of the child's biological sex. A female teacher gives rewards to a male child more often when he engages in feminine behavior than when he engages in masculine behavior. This is a great source of stress to the male child, who is still expected to retain his male sexual identity. While the child's male peers and his father help counter-act the teacher's effect, the teacher's behavior can pro-duce a great number of conflicts and problems for the male child.

The essence of this chapter has been to point out a major problem source in the sexual identity development of the child. As is evident, this problem source seems more prone to affect the boy than the girl.

VII.
The Masculinized Classroom

The feminine atmosphere that prevails in the elementary school is dependent upon two factors; the abundance of female teachers, and the rigid limits and restrictions necessary to maintain some control over such young individuals. As a child proceeds from elementary school to high school and perhaps to college, two interesting reversals occur. Teaching faculties become more and more dominated by males. And, as the students gain maturity, many rules and regulations become self-imposed, not enforced by outside authorities.

The young child was faced with a female who tried to instill, as a mother would do, certain basic and necessary skills that the child would find useful in later education. The youth is met by an adult male, who from a distance, gives advice and information; but who, like a father, expects the student to have already mastered the basics and leaves him to develop more or less on his own. The sequence in education is similar to what occurs in the family: the schools make a female the primary resource person and then introduce some male figures.

The child had been a largely passive recipient of information that had to be memorized by rote and regurgitated almost verbatim. Now he is expected to play an active role in the discovery and learning of knowledge. There is less memory work, and more need to apply basic principles in often abstract ways to relatively new problems. For example, the elementary school child learns that 2+2=4, and he memorizes that. The older student memorizes some basic algebraic principles with which he can solve numerous equations that contain unknowns.

The elementary school child is not to talk in class, even to borrow a pencil. If he perpetually carries on discussions with others, he is sent to the office and may even be physically punished. The university student is relatively free to talk all he wants. If he becomes obnoxious, his professor may ask for silence or his peers may cast discouraging glances, but overall there is little policing of the university students' verbal interactions in class.

In the elementary school, time limits are strictly enforced. School begins at 8:20 A.M., and if the child is not at his desk by then, his parents may receive a note. Recess is at 10:00 and the child had better not try to leave early, or even get ready to leave before the teacher says okay. Recess is over at 10:15, and when that bell rings, the child had better freeze in the yard and then proceed quietly to line up. And so it goes until the end of the day. In the university, times are mainly guidelines; observance of classtimes is expected more of teachers than of students. It is not uncommon to see university students strolling into class 10 minutes or so after the class has begun. Many professors start the proceedings some time after the class is scheduled in order to allow for these perpetually late students. Students also may walk out before the class is over, especially in large classes.

In elementary school, there is an emphasis on the individual student. If Johnny is not doing well, the teacher may try to find out why. She may work to help him herself or refer him for outside help. The university professor is less apt to do this—although the smaller the class, the more likely he is to at least take the student aside and talk to him. The fact is, the university professor is almost relieved to have such individuals in his class. It makes it easy for him to fill his quota of F's and D's.

The grading system also reverses in several ways. First, whereas in elementary school female teachers gave female pupils better grades even if the quality of their work was no better than that of males, it is now the male who receives the better grade, given equality of performance. This is so well documented that it is part of the reason that many professors prefer to grade their papers "blind" (i.e. not knowing which student wrote which paper).

Another grading system change is the shift from the predetermined standard to the comparative standard. To pass an elementary school reading test, for example, the child might have to obtain a predetermined score of 60 out of 65. In university, however, the grade is obtained by direct comparison with the scores of other students in the class. No matter how well or how poorly one does, his grade depends on how others do in relation to how he did. Students are thus placed in direct competition with one another. Many end up feeling, "It's them or me." Students assigned outside reading for a particular course have been known to steal the assigned materials so that others in the same course would be unable to read them and therefore would receive the poorer grades. Many students are ambivalent about giving fellow students help of any sort because they would essentially be aiding an enemy. Students quickly become indoctrinated into this system, and it endangers a true camaraderie and joint effort at academic success and learning.

Sexual Identity and Academic Success

One should be able to perceive the similarity between elementary school and the mother-child relationship, and the similarity between university and the father-child relationship. There is a drastic reversal from the feminized atmosphere of elementary school to the masculinized atmosphere of high school and especially university. It is no wonder, then, that many males do much better in higher educational levels than they do in the primary grades. And it is no wonder that many females, outstanding students in the primary grades, have difficulty maintaining average grades in high school and university. And, of course, it is no wonder that, whereas girls outshone boys before, the males in later grades are usually the more academically outstanding.

There are actually two proposed reasons for this. One is the hypothesis suggested here, which is that elementary school and later education have different requirements for success. The two approaches happen to divide along traditional gender-role lines. The other hypothesis rests on the differential maturational rates of males and females. In the primary grades, females are more mature physically, emotionally, socially, and intellectually. By the time high school and university roll around, the male has caught up with and surpassed the female. Hence, according to this hypothesis, differential rates of academic success reflect differential maturational levels of the two sexes.

There is a relatively easy way to check these two hypotheses. If the first hypothesis is true, masculine individuals, regardless of biological sex, should excel in high school and university. Feminine individuals, whether male or female, should do poorly. If the different maturational rate is the key, the difference in academic success should depend more on biological sex than on psychological sex, or sexual identity.

Data collected to date seem to support the sexual identity hypothesis. Many studies have examined boys whose fathers are absent. It is assumed that, on the average, such boys are more impaired in their masculine identity than are boys whose fathers are present. However, this assumption should be tempered with the realization that father-absent boys can have appropriate sexual identities, particularly if there has been some other male figure in the child's life. And, to a somewhat lesser degree, the child might avoid sexual identity problems if his mother tends to be somewhat masculine.

Nonetheless, the studies show father-absent boys to be at a decided disadvantage in higher education. Their ability to concentrate, plan ahead, and delay gratification is impaired. Their academic success is less than that of their male peers. Part of this seems related to the fact that they do not have a typical male motivation. For example, males with fathers absent during childhood possess a lower achievement motivation and have less career success than do males whose fathers were present (McClelland 1961).

Other studies have shown that even boys with fathers present may have problems. However, in this group, the boy who has a disturbed relationship with his father seems most likely to have problems. Reuter and Biller (1973) reported that college males who had nurturant fathers, as determined by self-reports, attained better scores on personality adjustment tests than did males who described their fathers as low in nurturance. Also, several studies have suggested that males from homes wherein the mother dominates tend to be more academically unsuccessful.

Even more impressive is the evidence that a close and warm father-daughter relationship helps develop in the girl autonomy, achievement, and independence. All of these are typically more masculine traits, but also, all of them are of great benefit for academic success in high school and college.

I briefly introduced this idea in Chapter 4 when the relationship between psychopathology and sexual identity was discussed. As was suggested then, a stable sexual identity is basic to the development of a stable and healthy personality. Inappropriate sexual identity, especially in the adolescent, can lead to confusion and poor psychosocial adjustment. At the same time, we have seen that a masculine sexual identity, or at least a masculine gender role, tends to be associated with achievement striving and academic success. So it seems that feminine males may be impaired both psychologically and academically. Masculine females may be impaired psychologically, but feminine females may be impaired academically. All this suggests that psychological and academic adjustment to high school and college may be harder for females than for males.

The Masculinized Classroom and Emotional Problems

High school and even junior high school, as the transition between elementary school and college, form a particularly important period in the adolescent's development. It is at this time that puberty strikes the child, and he is under a great deal of pressure related to sexual maturation. Girls begin to menstruate and may "sit out" gym classes. Boys' voices begin to change, and they may be embarrassed to speak in class. Common shower facilities make apparent to any roving eye one's comparative rate of sexual maturation. This may become a source of embarrassment and dismay.

Many high school students develop psychological problems associated with their sexual identity. Fears of attending school, demonstrated by shool phobias and truancies, may be particularly acute in youngsters whose earlier confusion in their sexual identity makes it difficult for them now to adopt the clearly defined gender roles being assumed by their peers. Further the youngster whose poor preparation for individuation includes uncertainty about sexual identity or fears of a heterosexual relationship may experience acute anxiety when his peers begin to structure their school life to include boy-girl relationships.

In the field of heterosexual relationships, there is strong evidence that, again, sexual identity is more important for the male than for the female. Seyfried and Hendrick (1973) examined the relationship between interpersonal attraction and sexual identity, or, more specifically, gender role. They gave university students descriptions of hypothetical individuals. Some of the descriptions were of masculine individuals (both male and female) and some were of feminine individuals (both male and female). The students then filled out a questionnaire dealing with their reactions to the individuals they read about. Male students were fairly unselective. Their attraction to a female was independent of the female's gender role. That is to say, males found masculine and feminine females equally attractive. Females, however, had a decided preference for masculine males. They were significantly more attracted to a masculine male than to a feminine male. Apparently, an appropriate sexual identity maximizes a male's interpersonal attractiveness. Feminine males are disadvantaged when they attempt to initiate and maintain a heterosexual relationship. Such a male not only would be less attractive to a female, but may be unable to adequately carry out his role, since our society still burdens the male with being the initiator and aggressor in heterosexual relations. The female, however, may or may not be the initiator and aggressor. She can start relationships with very little adverse effects, since males equally accept masculine and feminine females. If she does not initiate relationships, her behavior is still in line with her female gender role, so that she suffers no consequences other than to wait for some male to initiate a relationship with her. So, in terms of heterosexual relationships, only the feminine male seems at a disadvantage.

This probably leads to a great deal of frustration for the feminine male. In a recent study of over 300 individu-

als, I was unable to determine a difference in the sexual
interest of males with a masculine gender role and males
with a feminine gender role. It appears that masculine
and feminine males have similar levels of sexual interest
and probably of sexual drive. But the feminine male
tends to be the more frustrated, since his inappropriate
gender role adoption cuts down on his heterosexual
relationships.

This line of reasoning leads to an interesting speculation. Femininity in a male results in a certain amount of
heterosexual isolation. Such isolation could have two effects. First, it could have the same effect that it does on
forced heterosexual isolates such as prisoners and sailors.
That is, with heterosexual outlets blocked, and with
normal sex drive, the male may be more inclined to accept
homosexual outlets. Male homosexuals proba-
bly make more passes at males than do female heterosexuals. Hence, a passive male would have more opportunities for a sexual outlet with other males than with
females. This suggests that some homosexuality may
result, not from femininity in a male, but from heterosexual isolation produced by the femininity. While this proposition is only speculative, it gains modest support from
clinical work with homosexuals. Behavior therapists
claim they can increase their success in changing homosexual behavior to heterosexual behavior by adding assertiveness training and/or social skills training to the other
therapeutic procedures.

Another possible effect of heterosexual isolation is to
sharply limit the number of friends, associates, and ac-
quaintances a person might have. This means the individual can resort to few people in times of stress or need,
and is therefore more vulnerable to pressures than most
people are. As a result, psychopathology is more probable. It is not surprising, then, that some psychopathological groups, most notably schizophrenics and particularly the males in these groups, are less often married
and report less adequate heterosexual relationships than
do people drawn from the population at large.

This discussion is relevant to the subject of the masculinized classroom because (1) heterosexual relationships begin to occur during the time that the classroom becomes masculinized, and (2) the combination of the masculine classroom and heterosexual relationship formation puts an inordinate amount of pressure on the feminine male. The masculine male should do well in both the classroom and heterosexual relationships. The feminine female may suffer in class, but she should be able to resort to a heterosexual relationship to alleviate some of her classroom-related pressures.

Indirect support for this thesis comes from data that Heilbrun (1973) collected over a number of years. He tested university students who were seeking the aid of a counselling center. Such a center normally attracts individuals with academic or emotional problems or both. He consistently found that males who sought such help had usually identified themselves with a feminine parent. Hence, femininity in a male seems to endanger both academic and emotional well-being. However, over the years, he could find no such clear-cut relationship for females seeking such help. Had he examined his counselling group with respect to whether the problem was clearly academic or clearly emotional, he might have found that femininity in a female is associated with academic problems and masculinity in a female with emotional problems.

High school and especially college are environments that stress independence, ambition, assertiveness, competitiveness, self-sufficiency, self-reliance, and determination. These are all traditionally masculine traits. There should be no doubt that an individual lacking these characteristics is at an academic disadvantage. Feminine individuals often lack such traits and they are, more often than their masculine counterparts, the ones who develop academic problems leading to school disinterest, poor grades, dropping out of school, emotional pressures or various displacement activities (e.g. joining radical groups, extracurricular activities).

Displacement activities give the student a chance to excel at something other than academics or else provide a good "excuse" for not doing well in classwork. Many such students rationalize, "I could do much better at schoolwork if I didn't have to spend so much time on the school newspaper."

We might do well to identify, early in the school year, male adolescents who are feminine and to intervene with scholastic and psychological aid. This could put such students on the right foot before serious problems occur. Otherwise, the odds are against their successfully completing a college degree without academic or emotional problems.

Summary

As a child progresses from elementary school into high school and college, an interesting reversal occurs in his school environment. The classroom setting, overwhelmingly feminine in elementary school, becomes masculinized. Teaching faculties, dominated by women in the primary grades, include more and more men. Competition intensifies because students are graded not by a predetermined standard but against one another. Positive response to a competitive stimulus is a well-known male trait. If a male has a feminine identity, not only does his self-concept suffer, but his academic success may also be impaired. The female may be hampered in one of two ways. If her sexual identity is too masculine, her psychological well-being is in jeopardy. And if her identity is too feminine, she may do poorly academically.

VIII.
The Feminized
Mental Institution

In one of the studies I recently completed with Maxine Endman and Ilona Gossmann (LaTorre, Endman, and Gossmann 1976), we noted that both the male and female psychiatric patients had more-feminine scores than did a group of controls who were not psychiatric patients. The difference between the two groups of males was more striking than that between the two female groups. After some thought-provoking discussions, it was suggested that the inappropriate gender role associated with psychopathology may have been modified by a hospital environment that produced a more feminine gender role among patients. If so, the male patients' already feminine sexual identity would be further feminized, but the female patients' somewhat masculine sexual identity would be neutralized.

After even more discussions and many opportunities to observe ward routine, we were able to discern some of the feminizing influences inherent in a psychiatric inpatient care setting.

Personnel

We noted, first, the personnel. The average ward staff (in contrast to that depicted in the film *One Flew Over the Cuckoo's Nest*) consisted of a half-dozen female caretakers (usually psychiatric nurses) who were on duty all day and interacted with each patient more consistently than did any other staff member.

Patients often participated in certain activities aimed toward releasing them from the hospital and making them useful members of the community. One such activity, occupational therapy, is staffed almost exclusively by females. Another activity consists of interviews with social workers. They help solve problems in the patient's family that may adversely affect the patient. They also help to reestablish the patient in the community. In many hospitals, most of the social workers are female.

Males, however, do predominate in the upper echelons of staff. Of course, the higher the individual's status, the less time he spends with individual patients. For example, each ward has a chief-of-service or a physician-in-charge, a psychiatrist, who shoulders the responsibility of the ward. For a recent study, I contacted 23 wards from 6 hospitals in the Montreal area. All of the chiefs, without exception, were males. In contrast, 22 of the 23 head nurses were females. Needless to say, the head nurse spent more time in the ward than did the chief psychiatrist and she also interacted more with the patients.

Many wards also have psychiatric residents or psychiatrists-in-training. They work under the chief psychiatrist, usually see the patients more than he does, and are actually the ones responsible for the individual patients. The majority of psychiatric residents are males.

Patients *are* seen by psychiatric residents and

psychiatric chiefs. However, the time of these professionals must be divided among administrative duties, several inpatients, possibly private patients, possibly research, training (reading, seminars, supervision), and rounds. And so it is not uncommon to find inpatients complaining that they have not seen their doctors enough or even that they have only seen the doctor for an hour or so each week. This has become particularly true with the advent of chemotherapy. Much of the psychiatrists' efforts are now directed at determining the proper type and dosage of medication, which can be administered by the nursing staff. This is not to be viewed as a "cop out" by psychiatrists, for many studies have shown that, for several types of psychiatric disorders, chemotherapy achieves better and quicker results than psychotherapy, milieu therapy, or shock treatment.

In positions at the top of the hierarchy—clinical director, professional director, medical director—males predominate. And, of course, these males are even more removed from direct interaction with the patients than are the psychiatric residents and chiefs.

So what is the problem with having so many female staff members continually interacting with the patients? We have noted already that one study demonstrated that female teachers reinforce feminine behavior in a child irrespective of the child's biological sex. One of the hypotheses put forth in that study was that people tend to reinforce behaviors that are in their own repertoire and fail to reinforce behaviors dissimilar to their own. Female teachers, having more feminine attributes than masculine attributes, reinforce femininity. In fact, any female, provided she has more feminine than masculine attributes, reinforces femininity more than masculinity. And, conversely, males reinforce masculinity more than femininity.

In psychiatric hospitals, the patient is reinforced more often for feminine behavior than for masculine behavior. This is true because the ward reinforcers, the staff members, are predominantly female. These same staff members also serve the patient as models of normal or adjusted behavior. As children try to emulate their teacher's behavior, so too may the psychiatric patient try to emulate his caretakers' behavior. This should be all right for the female patient but may pose serious problems for the male. As shown in Chapter 4, male psychiatric patients may already be alienated from their apropriate sexual identity. The psychiatric ward may undermine the patient's sexual adjustment even more. If an alienated sexual identity helps cause psychological maladjustment then confinement may actually work against long-term recovery.

Peers

In the school environment, the male child's peers, particularly the other boys, seemed to help him resist the teacher's inappropriate reinforcement of feminine behavior. The little contact that the male patient has with male staff might also help, but such contact is minimal. The other source of reinforcement is fellow patients. But even this source is less than ideal, for two reasons. First, male psychiatric patients seem to have more feminine qualities than they should. If they have feminine qualities, they also reinforce such qualities in others. Second, it is a consistent finding that except in Veteran's Administration Hospitals female patients outnumber male patients. Hence, not only are there more female than male staff members, but there are more female than male patients. The male psychiatric patient is surrounded by female staff, female patients, and less than typically masculine male patients. All reinforce a somewhat feminine behavioral pattern.

Hospital Routine

The psychiatric patient is further pressured into a role that is more feminine than masculine by the necessities of ward routine. Like a schoolboy, the patient is placed in a role of submissiveness, dependence, and obedience. The "manly" qualities of aggression, assertion, and swearing are naturally discouraged, if not punished outright. This is not brought about by any malice on the part of the staff. More feminine attributes appear to be necessary to safeguard the patient from himself, to safeguard patients from one another, to make the lives of staff members a little more bearable, and to keep chaos from reigning.

I recently witnessed the following situation, which exemplifies much of this discussion. A patient refused (masculinity) to take his medication from a female nurse. The nurse retreated (femininity) to the nursing station and informed the head nurse. The head nurse went out with the other nurse and asked (femininity) the patient to take his medicine. "I don't need it," said the patient, "I'm okay now." "Well, you don't look okay," said the head nurse. The patient still did not take the medication. "Okay," the head nurse warned, "if you don't take it yourself, then I call four men to hold you down and we'll give it to you in an injection!" Eventually the patient will have to yield (femininity). Obviously, it is good for a patient to take his medication (assuming, of course, that he isn't a political prisoner or that the nurses are not involved in some illegal conspiracy). However, the psychiatric patient's role—even if it is for his own good—is more feminine than masculine. And despite the good that comes from it, it can also produce problems of its own.

The psychiatric ward and the psychiatric institution are themselves societies. And, like any other society, they can affect the behavior of the people who are a part of them. The institutional society seems to be most similar to a type of strong maternalism.

William Caudill, an anthropologist who simulated mental illness so as to be admitted to a psychiatric hospital, has written a book about the hospital as a society (1958). His vivid and intriguing descriptions of events impart the feminizing flavor of ward routine.

He discusses, for example, a patient whom he calls Mr. Esposito. During his first day in the hospital, Mr Esposito was assured by his therapist that "he was in a hospital where he would be taken care of." So a feminine, dependent role was already offered to him. He also learned that when he was cooperative (which often meant sleeping) the staff was happy with him. When he was not cooperative, he was punished. Disagreements with the night nurse resulted in his being put in seclusion. Thus, a yielding or passive feminine role was reinforced. Several times, Mr. Esposito woke up in the night and asked for a cigarette. In response, the nurses gave him extra sedation, which was their attempt to force him into the ward routine of sleep between ten and six.

One night he came out of his room to ask for a cigarette. A nurse started to escort him to his room, so he started to hop. Because he hopped, he was put in seclusion, where he started to masturbate. When he started to masturbate, he was given chloral hydrate (a sedative). It is apparent that each of this patient's attempts to assert himself was met with disapproval or even punishment.

Caudill also gives us some insight into how a patient's peer group (other patients) can influence his behavior. Mr. Esposito developed a friendship with another male patient. Mr. Esposito, while imitating much of the patient's behavior, actually put a lot of pressure on the other patient to stop talking and swearing so much.

In his early days of hospitalization, Mr. Esposito repeatedly exposed himself. This probably served much the same purpose as other exhibitionism. Mr. Esposito was put into an environment that treated him femininely. By exposing himself, he was trying to say to everyone, "Hey, look, I'm a man so treat me like one!"

Of course, Mr. Esposito was not released until his behavior stabilized and conformed with the staff's expectations of "normal" behavior. The behavior that the staff expects is normal for a psychiatric patient about to be discharged, which is considerably more feminine than the norm as defined by people who are not hospitalized. For example, Mr. Esposito had orders from his doctor that he was to be allowed to go on the unlocked ward as often as he wished. Yet he was turned down by two orderlies when he asked to go. He did not assert himself but passively retired to his room. This is quite a different response from the type seen when he was admitted eight weeks previously.

The above examples should shed some light on how the psychiatric hospital can induce a feminine orientation in a patient. He is given three meals a day plus snacks. He has a place to stay. He does not go out to work in order to earn money to take care of himself. All of his needs, except sexual, are the responsibility of the hospital. The patient follows a routine that begins early in the morning. Meals are at specified times, he takes medication at specified times, ward activities follow a routine, the patient has a schedule for such activities as occupational therapy, and so it goes until the specified time that the patient is expected to retire.

There is little chance for the patient to display masculine qualities. Let us compare a possible day outside the hospital with a day within the hospital. Outside the hospital, the individual is responsible for beginning his day. He has to get up and get ready to go to work. He may be responsible for preparing his own breakfast. In contrast, the hospital patient is awakened by the staff and has no choice but to rise. Many never take care of their personal hygiene throughout the entire day. Breakfast is prepared for them. Even the dishes are done by others.

The nonhospitalized person is responsible for getting to work on time. He gains a certain amount of satisfaction from feelings of competency regarding his job. The job itself has many responsibilities and probably carries some authority. Even though he has a supervisor who expects a certain work output, the person is relatively autonomous in getting that work done

In contrast, the hospital patient must do whatever

the hospital thinks is best for him. Some days he may have several activities scheduled—for example, occupational therapy, industrial therapy, and small group meetings. Other days, there may be absolutely nothing planned for him, so that he must stay on the ward, sleeping, watching television, talking with others, or possibly just sitting. He has little responsibility and absolutely no authority. If the authorities say he stays in his room, he does so. If they send him to some activity, he goes. He has little or no say in what would be best for his recovery.

The man on the outside has a number of choices for his evening activities. He can go home, have a drink, and eat dinner. He can go out for drinks and try to meet new people. He can go out for dinner. He can look into some entertainment, such as a show or a play. He can decide to go to a discotheque. He can decide anything, and he can do it. The patient, on the other hand, can do just one thing. He can stay around the ward. Possibly friends or relatives visit him, but he cannot go visit them. Unless he has visitors, his evening is spent with the other patients and the night staff. No matter what he would like to do, he can only spend another evening on the ward.

The nonpatient controls his own life right up to the time that he chooses to go to bed. The patient has his life dictated to him right up to the time that he must go to bed. Should the nonpatient awaken in the night and want a cigarette, a drink, or food, he can have it. No one controls this but himself. But, as we saw with the example of Mr. Esposito, the patient is expected to sleep throughout the night. And no deviations are accepted.

Discharge from the Hospital

This consistent picture of dependency, passivity, and deference is actually counterproductive, for the following reason. As we saw with Mr. Esposito, the less a patient deviates from the feminine attributes desirable for ward-management, the greater are his chances for discharge. Hence, an atypical gender role adoption is often taken as a sign that the person is ready for the outside world. However the outside world often requires more-masculine attributes from a person. The feminine types of behavior required for discharge from the hospital may, in fact, be hazardous to the patient's success in the community.

So the hospital is actually training the person to behave in a way that will not help him too much and may actually hurt him after discharge. It is no surprise, then, that a "revolving door" phenomenon exists. It is not uncommon that a person who has been admitted to a mental hospital and discharged will be back again in a matter of days, weeks, months, or possibly years. Many patients seem to shuttle back and forth between the hospital and the outside as if they were stuck in a revolving door that turned around on the outside and brought them back inside the institution.

The revolving door phenomenon is easily explicable from the discussion presented above. A person prepared to react to life situations with feminine responses will obviously fail in situations that require masculine responses. And feminine responses are encouraged when patients are cared for, are told how to live their lives, and have only one responsibility: to do what they are told. But upon release, men are placed into the community with little support. They are not awakened by someone else; they do not have their breakfast made for them; people do not watch over them to make sure they are doing all right. They are on their own, independent, responsible, and once again men.

Such a patient may have to go out and find a job or return to one he previously had. His boss and coworkers do not care for him as did the hospital staff. He may get special consideration for a time, but he will eventually have to perform, or else he will be replaced. In short, he is

put in a competitive situation for his job. Having been
encouraged by the psychiatric setting to take a dependent role, he may compare poorly with some go-getter who
is seeking the same job.

The Patient's Life Cycle

Overall for the male patient the picture looks something like this. From his very early years, his mother and
father have raised him in a family environment that jeop-
ardized his masculine sexual identity. His mother may
have been overly close and refused him any independence. His father may have been a poor role model or may
have retreated emotionally or physically from the family,
leaving the son to become even closer to the mother and to
value her femininity.

With his masculine sexual identity already in jeopardy, he is placed in a school setting with, again, a female
as the central adult figure. She also reinforces his
feminine qualities. A peer group may be his only chance
at recovery, since his father plays such a small part in his
life. However, if he conforms to his peer group's pressures, he risks losing his mother's love. So he gives in to
his mother and teacher. He may very well excel in
academics, but he may end up with few or no friends. He
may be the apple of his mother's eye and a teacher's pet,
but he certainly is not Mr. Popular with his peers.

Next, he enters high school, an increasingly masculine environment. He once could at least take pride in his
school work, but now he finds himself only an average
scholar. School becomes less and less positively valued.
His feminine orientation also makes him unattractive to
his adolescent peers, both male and female. His feminine orientation also inhibits an active attempt to find
friends. At a time when the family is becoming less important, and the peer group more important, he has few
or no friends to help him with his transition to manhood
and independence. His heterosexual relations are also
impaired. With many of his peers bragging about "mak-

ing out," he may have a growing feeling that he is lacking in a certain virility or manhood. He begins to withdraw more and more from a life that seems to have an increasing number of pressures.

The individual becomes ill equipped for survival in a society that expects the male to be the aggressive, independent, self-sufficient cornerstone of his own family. In fact, he is even ill equipped to start a family. Continually meeting new pressures requiring masculine responses, the individual comes closer and closer to his vulnerability level. And we know what awaits him if he crosses his level of vulnerability.

Once he requires professional assistance, and particularly if he is hospitalized, his sexual identity, already alienated or confused, is met by strong feminizing influences. He is surrounded by female caretakers and female copatients. He probably sees the patient role as more feminine than masculine if for no other reason than the predominance of female patients. Staff members place him in a dependent and subordinate position, a role that actually helped lead to his hospitalization in the first place.

And amazingly, when he has been sufficiently socialized within his psychiatric patient role, when he has demonstrated to all that he can do what he is told without giving anyone problems, when he has exhibited a sufficient amount of ability to control his wants and desires, when he has shown that he can exist without aggression—then the hospital may decide to discharge. He is ready for the outside. But not really. What he is actually ready for is "patienthood."

Back in society, his patienthood brings numerous problems unless he has a maternal boss or still lives with his mother. Otherwise, it interferes with a successful, readjustment to society, which is often described as a "jungle." Certainly, this person is more of a Jane than a Tarzan—and so has little chance.

It is more than likely that he will resort to his patienthood over and over, whenever the "jungle" gets too tough. The hospital serves as a "time out" from the many pressures in society. It is a place wherein he can attain a certain success by enacting a role that has been a part of his being since his earliest years.

The movie *One Flew Over the Cuckoo's Nest,* centered on a group of patients on a psychiatric ward. The main character, played by Jack Nicholson, was certainly the most masculine of the patients—a fact made apparent in several scenes. Those traits that made him the most masculine patient also made him the "worst" patient. Yet, of all the patients, he seemed to be the one best equipped for survival on the outside. He was in charge of the fishing trip. He taught the others how to fish, how to run the boat. And they succeeded in bringing back a good catch. Certainly it was also his more masculine attributes that made him cross the law. And it was this act that resulted in his hospitalization and eventual lobotomy. Cutting parts of his brain was akin to castrating a bull to make him a docile work ox.

Outsiders' and Insiders' Views

As a coup de grace, I would like to present some preliminary findings of a study currently in progress. These results have not yet been published. In order to assess the validity of our hypothesis that a psychiatric hospital tends to make one conform to a role that is more feminine than masculine, we asked a number of individuals to complete a special questionnaire. The male and female items from the BSRI (discussed in Chapter III) were used. Instead of rating *themselves* on the 40 items, people rated how desirable each trait would be for a psychiatric patient. Four groups were asked to complete this questionnaire: recently hospitalized schizophrenics, recently hospitalized manic depressives, schizophrenics hospitalized for a number of years, and individuals who had never been admitted to a psychiatric hospital.

Specifically, the three patient groups were asked to

rate how desirable or undesirable the ward staff would find each of the 40 items if a patient exhibited that attribute. The nonpatient controls were asked to rate how desirable or undesirable the staff of a psychiatric institution would find the attributes if they were displayed by a patient in their charge. The rating scale consisted of seven points with "always desirable" at one end and "always undesirable" at the other end.

The nonpatient individuals rated the feminine attributes as almost one whole point more desirable than the masculine attributes. Both schizophrenic groups expressed a belief that feminine behaviors were more desirable than masculine behaviors. Only the manic-depressive group believed that masculine behaviors were more appreciated by the staff. This group scored the lowest difference in desirability ratings between the masculine and feminine behaviors—about one-tenth of a point.

This study is interesting for two reasons. First, using nonpatient normal controls who have never had a psychiatric hospitalization, we can assess the stereotypes of appropriate psychiatric patient behavior. The result serves as an index of how people think patients should behave on a ward if they wish to please the staff. And, more importantly, it tells us what self-imposed behavioral expectancies an outsider will bring into the hospital if he is ever admitted. For even before the staff begins its socialization of the patient, the patient has his own schema of "good" behavior, which apparently tends to be more feminine than masculine in nature.

Secondly, the study gives us an insider's view of what good behavior includes. The insiders in the study are the three patient groups. They, too, believe that good ward behavior is slightly more feminine than masculine, or that feminine attributes are slightly more appreciated than masculine attributes.

Of course, patients' perceptions could be distorted, and the stereotypes of outsiders are just stereotypes. It

would be extremely interesting to have ward staff fill out
the questionnaire and to see if their definition of desirable ward behavior is more similar to masculinity or
femininity. I had envisioned such a study at one time, but
ward staff had little time available for it, and, in any
case, they were reluctant to allow anyone to assess their
attitudes, so the project was abandoned.

It would be of even greater interest to observe actual
transactions on the ward to see when patients are reinforced and for what activities or behaviors. Examining
the results in terms of masculine or feminine activities
and behaviors could give us further valuable information.

At present, it does seem probable that the psychiatric institution exerts a feminizing influence on its patients. This is relevant, as many patients, particularly
males, have a sexual identity problem already. Such a
state of affairs would also help explain the high readmit-
tance rate. What, if anything, should be done about this
will be discussed in Chapter 11.

Summary

Considering that psychopathology is associated
with, and may be caused by, an impaired sexual identity,
it is not encouraging, for males at least, to find a
feminized atmosphere in the psychiatric hospital. Most of
the people who have the most patient contact are females.
They include the psychiatric nurses, physiotherapists,
occupational therapists, and social workers. Males in the
hospital tend to hold administrative positions and have
little direct patient contact. Furthermore, it is known that
females outnumber males in mental hospitals. So, not
only are most authority figures females, but most of the
patient's peers are also females. Finally, it is well known
psychiatric hospitals encourage female characteristics of
passivity and dependence more than male characteristics of assertiveness and independence.

IX.

The Feminized Psychotherapeutic Relationship

Previous chapters have dealt with sexual identity and with the relationship between sexual identity and psychopathology (i.e. psychological maladjustment or mental illness). Studies have fairly conclusively demonstrated that, for males, a faulty or inappropriate sexual identity is often associated with psychopathology. This is true whether one defines psychopathology in terms of psychiatric hospitalization or in terms of scores obtained on tests of psychological adjustment.

It is ironic that, when an individual's maladjustment is severe enough to warrant hospitalization, he is thrust into an environment that influences him to behave more femininely than masculinely. If anything, at that point in time, the male needs reassurance of his male sexual identity. He needs to have appropriate male role models. He needs to be encouraged to display more masculine behaviors and to feel confident in doing so. He

needs to be reinforced for a masculine gender role
adoption.

But what of the person who is less than optimally adjusted, who may even be classified as psychopathological but who is not hospitalized? Might it not actually be
better for an individual to try to obtain psychiatric aid
from a personal therapist rather than expose himself to a
psychiatric team in a hospital? Perhaps not. It is the
thesis of this chapter that even psychotherapy demands
a feminine orientation from the client.

Complementarity

As female psychologists in the feminist movement
are quick to point out, the majority of psychotherapists
are male. Now, after the long discussion concerning the
overabundance of female staff in psychiatric institutions and the resulting feminizing effect, many readers
are probably thinking, "Then psychotherapy must exert a
masculinizing effect." Certainly, to be consistent, I must
admit that the therapist, being a male, tends to reinforce
his client more for masculine than for feminine behaviors. For example, he may smile when the client tells him
she told off her husband; he may remain silent or give a
scornful glance when the client tells him that she got
shortchanged in a restaurant and did nothing about it.

However, the psychotherapeutic relationship, unlike
the institutional one, is a one-to-one relationship. It is
basically two individuals in interaction. And when only
two people are involved, something peculiar happens.
They do not mimic each other or follow cne another's
example. Instead of becoming similar, the two people
become complementary to each other. Hence, if one person
is assertive, the other, instead of also being assertive,
tends to become passive. This is almost by necessity. It is
unlikely that two individuals exactly alike could maintain
a working relationship. If one is a talker, the other should
be a listener. Two talkers become frustrated, and two
listeners are like two logs. If one is dominant, the other

should be yielding. Two dominant persons become a threat to each other, and two yielding persons can never even get through a door because each keeps trying to yield the right of way to the other.

Hence, if the therapist is a male and has a masculine gender role adoption, a client may in many respects become the complement and adopt some feminine gender roles. If a client does not complement the therapist in certain respects, the therapeutic relationship is almost certainly doomed. It is not uncommon for a therapist to dislike a client or a client to dislike a therapist. And research has demonstrated that dislike of one another results in slower progress; in a number of cases, dissolution of the relationship becomes necessary. I should like to suggest that the basis for such incompatibility is often the failure of the therapist and client to complement each other in one or more of several important areas related to sexual identity. On the other hand, it appears that similarity is essential with respect to intelligence, social class, and race.

Patient Roles

So what are some of the areas of complementarity that are also related to gender roles? Probably one of the basic requirements in psychotherapy is that the client be verbal or expressive. The therapist, often to the frustration of the client, is the silent partner. The entire burden falls on the client. He must disclose his problems, he must express his feelings, he must almost carry on a running monologue. The therapist's part varies depending on his "school." If he is a traditional analyst, he may say nothing during many sessions and may not even let the client face him during discussions. If he is a humanist, he tries to reflect the client's feelings or offer small acknowledgments that he is in touch with what the client is saying. At any rate, few psychotherapists, except possibly during an initial session, try to extract information from a client with a series of questions, nor will a therapist give his own personal reactions or self-disclosures related to the topic areas the client offers. This situation is reminiscent of the breakfast table scene shown in television and movies. The wife is carrying on a running monologue while the husband, with head buried in the newspaper, offers at best an occasional acknowledgment that, yes, he is listening.

It is, in our society, the female role to be the verbal one. From infancy on, there is evidence that the female excels in verbal skills. Her edge over the male continues throughout life, from childhood to adulthood. Often people have noted that the female is born with the "gift of gab." The verbosity of the female has often been the target of ridicule in cartoons and other media.

Associated with verbalness is self-disclosure. The client is required to tell all. He is to be completely honest with the therapist. Certainly the therapist allows the client sufficient time to disclose his innermost thoughts, conflicts, and problems. I remember one case in which, after several months of therapy, a male client said, "By the way, I don't know if I told you this, but I think my problem is that I'm a homosexual." This person never even gave me an indication of his homosexuality until this disclosure, and yet he defined it as his "problem."

In order to facilitate self-disclosure, essential for therapeutic progress, professionals are ethically required to keep confidential the information disclosed to them by a client. Without self-disclosure, no matter how verbal the client, therapy will go nowhere. Verbalness without self-disclosure is no more than a casual social interaction. The client must disclose even, and sometimes particularly, those things that may cause embarrassment or pain.

Again we find that this therapy role is usually one attributed to the female in our society. It is consistently found in research studies that the female is more self-disclosing than the male (Cozby 1973). This concept has already been introduced in Chapter IV.

So it would seem that females are better suited for

self-disclosure than are males. It is uncertain how this difference in willingness to reveal personal information comes about. Perhaps it is related to parents' trying to teach their sons to "keep a stiff upper lip" or not to be a "stool pigeon." Perhaps it is related to the little boy's being taught to fight his own battles while the little girl is encouraged to seek help. But whatever its roots, it is a fact that females self-disclose more than do males. And it is fact that psychotherapy requires self-disclosure. Hence, to make psychotherapy work, the male must adopt, for the time being at least, one more feminine characteristic.

Another role of the psychotherapeutic client is to be emotionally expressive. The therapist is interested in hearing the client talk (being verbal) and discuss problem areas (self-disclosure). He is also very interested in the client's feelings about various problems—that is, in emotional expression. The therapist wants to know that he is dealing with a human, a human with feelings. And he wants to know the feelings that are part of his client's inner being.

Many people who seek therapy are frustrated, have pent-up anger, are depressed, or are afraid of something. Sometimes people are afraid or anxious and don't know why. It is important to get at these feelings and to work with them. The client who told me he was a homosexual was actually telling me that he was ashamed of his homosexuality or that he was afraid that he might not be normal.

The therapy role of emotional expressiveness also fits better with the traditional female role than the traditional male role. As discussed in Chapter 2, females take the expressive role and males the instrumental role in all societies. So, all in all, it appears that a therapy client should possess certain feminine qualities.

A male comes to the therapy situation ill equipped for his new role. Throughout his life, he has been taught the antithesis of many of the qualities necessary for successful therapy. But he is expected to accomplish a reversal and suddenly become expressive, verbal, and self-disclosing. Certainly, this source of stress is unique to the male in therapy. The female entering therapy brings her feminine talents with her, and these are usually sufficient for the psychotherapy relationship.

The dissonance created by a situation that demands a role with which an individual has little experience can be called role strain. Roles within the psychotherapeutic relationship have been a focus for research during the last decade. One of the main problems noted involves role expectations. It was found that, when an individual's expectancies of the client role were discrepant with the actual client role, strain developed. And role strain interfered with therapeutic progress in one of several ways. The least harmful was that important time, which should have been devoted to therapy, was taken up as the client learned the appropriate role. One of the more severe results was that the client took himself out of the role strain by discontinuing therapy.

This research has direct application to our current discussion. Role strain should be more evident in the male client than in the female client. The male entering psychotherapy, with its femine demands, finds the setting more unfamiliar than the female does. Therefore, it takes more valuable time to settle the male into the proper role than to settle the female into that role. One would expect more males than females to drop out early in the relationship. One would also predict that females would benefit more, or more quickly, from psychotherapy.

These are not idle speculations. There are data to support some of these statements. Several reports acknowledge that females respond better to psychotherapy than do males. Not only is it true that females have better outcomes, but also it is *expected* that they will fare better.

Societal Expectations

One study involved asking individuals if, after they

had read a case history of a schizophrenic, they believed the individual needed care and what type of care would be needed. They were also asked how much benefit the schizophrenic could expect to receive from that care. Case histories were presented so that some individuals read the case history of a male and others read the *same* case history but of a female. Only the individual's sex was changed. Those who believed psychotherapy was needed predicted a better outcome for the female than for the male (LaTorre 1975). This is particularly striking since the symptomatology was exactly the same for both sexes. The sex of the client alone elicited different expectations of outcome. It could very well be that most people realize that psychotherapy elicits a feminine role orientation and that it will be easier for a female to comply. As a result, the female will benefit more.

The attempt to attain psychotherapeutic aid, or any outside help, is itself seen as a somewhat feminine gesture. The male is, of course, expected to solve his own problems. Remember the mother pushes the infant male towards independence. And from then on, he is trained to solve his own problems. How many times has one heard, "If someone beats you up and you come crying to me, I'll wallop you myself . . . be a man and stick up for yourself . . . next time he pushes you, punch him in the nose!" These are things said to a male child by the father. But what happens if a little girl comes to daddy because Tommy hit her? Poor Tommy will be paid a visit by an irate daddy who may just break Tommy's neck.

As was true of psychiatric hospitalization, more females than males become involved in psychotherapy. Howard and Orlinsky (1972) attribute this phenomenon to the female's more positive attitude towards seeking aid and greater readiness to define personal problems within the context of psychiatric help. Howard and Orlinsky also note that, in consequence, males in psychotherapy are generally more seriously disturbed than are females who seek such help. Apparently a male avoids psychiatric help at all costs until it is absolutely necessary. A female more readily chooses this feminine alternative, even if she is just mildly disturbed.

That females are more readily allowed or expected to seek outside help was also confirmed in a study I completed (LaTorre 1975). More of the individuals questioned recommended psychiatric help for a female with certain symptons than for a male with the same symptons. Psychiatric care is seen as a feminine alternative. Males, apparently, are expected either not to have psychological problems or to cure themselves.

This whole conception of psychiatric care being a feminine alternative is probably partially responsible for the results obtained in outcome studies. Perhaps males entering psychotherapy begin to feel that they have forfeited their masculinity. They are no longer self-reliant, but interdependent. This may increase their problems and work against therapeutic progress. Females, on the other hand, may have their femininity reinforced in psychotherapy. Psychotherapy helps bolster an important area in their life. This would aid therapeutic progress.

Obviously, the relationship between the client's gender roles (or sexual identity in general) and psychotherapeutic process and outcome is an area ripe for experimental investigation. Of even further interest would be the relationship between the sexual identity of both the therapist and the client and the therapeutic process.

The Male in Therapy

It seems at this point I have talked myself into a contradiction. First, as noted in Chapter IV, the males likely to seek out psychotherapy may be slightly more feminine than other males. Second, as noted in this chapter, psychotherapy should run more smoothly for a person with feminine attributes. It would seem to follow, then, that psychotherapy should benefit the males who seek it out since they are femininely oriented; and even further, that such males should not do less well than females in therapy. While it is true that some males *do* benefit from psychotherapy, it is also true that they do less well than do females.

This discrepancy can be resolved in several ways. First, it is true that males seeking psychotherapy may be slightly more feminine than males not in therapy. However, females seeking psychotherapy may be more feminine than females not seeking therapy. This would mean that female clients are still more feminine than male clients and that they should, therefore, benefit more from psychotherapy.

Second, the greater femininity of male clients is determined by the specifics of sexual identity that are examined. Perhaps the specifics on which the male client is more feminine are not the specifics needed to do well in psychotherapy. That is, a male client may be more feminine than a male nonclient because he is not self-reliant, dominant, or assertive, but is yielding, eager to help others, and dependent. Yet, he may be no different from male nonclients for the specifics of verbalness, self-disclosure, and emotional expressiveness. The client's greater femininity is thus confined to a set of specifics that are not relevant to the requirements for a successful psychotherapeutic relationship. With regard to the specifics important for psychotherapy, he is as masculine as a nonclient male and more masculine than a client female. Therefore, he fares more poorly in psychotherapy than the female does.

A third explanation has been touched on briefly before. The male client comes to psychotherapy with a sexual identity problem. And the therapy situation itself may be seen as a threat to the masculinity the client does have. He is already concerned about his masculinity, and the psychotherapeutic situation may be an added threat. Naturally the male does poorly in such a situation if, in fact, he even remains in it.

The Female in Therapy

Until now we have dwelt almost exclusively on the

male. The female and psychotherapy would seem to be a good match. If she has somewhat unfeminine sexual identity, psychotherapy pressures her to become more feminine. She sees that femininity is accepted, and she becomes more confident about displaying it. In fact, sometimes individuals in therapy overgeneralize these qualities and display them outside the therapy situation. If you have ever known individuals who have been in psychotherapy, the chances are that you have noted that they tend to be more self-disclosing than most other people. Apparently their self-disclosure was met with such acceptance by the therapist that they try to gain the acceptance of others by using this same technique.

And what if the female comes to therapy with a sexual identity that is more feminine than average? Then she fits into the psychotherapeutic relationship as easily as a soapy finger slips into a ring. Therapy under such conditions should progress fairly smoothly.

In fact, about the only problem a female seems to have in psychotherapy is that most therapists are male. Some women believe that they cannot discuss certain things with a male therapist or that he will be unreceptive to certain feelings or ideas. Possibly this is true in some cases. Therapists are individuals. Their own opinions and attitudes certainly influence the course of therapy. But such a blanket statement, like all blanket statements, is false in many cases. The envisioned problems are often problems only in the females' minds.

One young female student had come to me for several months concerning an emotional problem that interfered with her schoolwork. At Christmas, she discontinued treatment. Several months later, she returned and asked to be referred to a female therapist. This surprised me since I felt that we had a fairly good relationship prior to the Christmas break. The explanation was that she had begun a homosexual relationship with her roommate during the interim and felt she would be unable to discuss lesbianism with a male therapist. I asked her to continue with me for a few sessions and promised to refer her to a female therapist if she did not feel she was making progress. By the end of a few months, not only was she continuing with me, but her roommate/lover had discontinued treatment with a female therapist, and together they came to me for counseling. It has been two years since they came, and I was fortunate to recently see one of them. They are still together.

Whether or not a person or his problems will be accepted by the therapist depends on the therapist himself and not the therapist's biological sex. In fact, research supports the idea that a better outcome can be expected for a female if her therapist is male. This may be so because the two participants play complementary roles, with the patient having the more feminine role. The female thus gains a chance to practice her femininity in an accepting and supporting environment.

Summary

Psychotherapy, like psychiatric hospitalization, may be a femininizing situation. The main criterion for psychotherapy is that the client be expressive. Expressiveness has long been noted as a central female trait. In addition, the client is dependent on the therapist and must accept the therapist's interpretations, task-oriented suggestions, and advice—however little of it the client may receive. It is no wonder, then, that females consistently benefit more from psychotherapy than do males.

X.
Implications of an Androgynous Society

Parsons and Bales, remember, divided behavior along an instrumental/expressive axis. They found that, throughout all societies, males clustered around the instrumental pole and females clustered about the expressive pole. This means that males are usually more involved in task-oriented functions. They take the initiative in insuring survival of the family against outside elements. They are responsible for housing and for bringing home food. They protect the female and children and insure the survival of their family, often at the risk of their own life. Observe, for example, the similarity between the native who goes out hunting a wild boar, the Eskimo who stalks the polar bear, and the businessman who must face rush-hour traffic!

The female normally is more expressive. Her functions include protecting the family from within. The husband may bring home the food, but she prepares it and feeds the family. The husband may fill some of her basic needs for food and shelter, but she must fulfill some of her husband's needs, too. She is, in a sense, the stabilizer of the family. She tends to be more person-oriented than the male. She is generally gentler and more patient. She usually is the primary caretaker of the children, and her more-subdued characteristics probably evolved because of her child-caring role.

But besides merely describing this state of affairs, Parsons and Bales went one step further and claimed that it was actually good for society. And this one step threw them into disrepute with the feminist movement. They believed in a simple principle: The more effort one puts into being X, the less effort one will be able to put into being Y. If one tries to be both X and Y, he will gain less ability at either one than someone who specializes in X or Y. Or, to paraphrase an old maxim, "A jack of all trades is master of none."

In addition, androgyny not only involves learning more, it entails learning to differentiate and being able to use these different sets of traits in different situations appropriately. A child will not only have to learn *how* to be aggressive and *how* to be passive, but will have to learn *when* to be aggressive and *when* to be passive.

Parsons and Bales's position actually makes sense. Take a look, for example, at the decathlon event in the Olympics. Each athlete must perform in ten different tests of skill. Would anyone arrange a discus match between a decathlon contestant and a discus specialist and expect a fair contest? Of course not. The training time a decathlon athlete spends on any one event necessarily takes away from the training devoted to the other events.

In our society, males and females are "trained" to excel in different areas. For example, the male is trained to excel in mathematical skills, and the female is trained in social skills. By this differentiation, society provides itself with both outstanding mathematical skills and well-developed social skills. But what if society trained males and females in all skills? The time males spent learning social skills would cut into the time they could devote to mathematics, (or some other male skill), and the time females spent on mathematics would deprive them of time for learning social skills (or some other female skill). With such training, each individual would have more skills to his credit, but, with the addition of each new skill, all other skills would suffer.

However, while this may be true, the feminist movement may still question why the female has to take on the expressive aspects of societal life while the male is taught instrumental qualities. Probably the simplest explanation is that, assuming society has equal need for expressive and instrumental qualities, the division of labor is most easily accomplished along male/female biological sex lines. Imagine if we were to try to train half the males and half the females to be instrumental, and the other half the males and half the females to be expressive. How would we achieve this? Would we draw lots at birth to see who should be which? After all, it appears that instrumental/expressive functioning, a part of sexual identity, is taught from birth onward. And then what about school and society at large? Would children wear badges proclaiming whether they were being reared to be insrtumental or to be expressive? It seems that biological sex is an efficient, although not necessarily fair, way of assigning individuals to an instrumental or expressive pole.

The placement of females toward the expressive pole actually made sense in primitive societies. Females, as the primary caretakers of children, were almost forced to develop a behavioral pattern different from that of males. The human infant is not as mobile as are the infants of lower animals; so it was necessary for mothers to stay around one central location. The male, on the other hand, went out to find food and fight battles. This division was useful for the community and, aided surely by evolution, was perpetuated into modern society—where it is possible that it is outdated.

In direct contradiction to Parsons and Bales's belief that specialization in society good, Bakan has argued against it. As you may recall, Bakan gave the terms agency and communion to roughly the same phenomena that Parsons and Bales labeled instrumental and expressive, respectively. Bakan believed that agency and communion were fundamental to *all* life. Agency specifically deals with the self as the center of attraction, while communion deals with the self as it is part of a larger group of individuals.

The extra step that Bakan ventured, however, met with approval from the feminist movement. He suggested that individual overspecialization in either agency or communion would eventually be to the detriment of society. He believed that agency and communion should coexist in each individual and that one should temper the other.

Some writers have carried Bakan's thinking even further. They believe that, for optimal functioning, each individual should have a *balance* of agency and communion, which become synonymous with masculinity and femininity, respectively (Bem 1975; Block 1973). It is argued that extremes of gender role adoption interfere with many aspects of the individual's life. Hyperpassivity interferes with a child's acquisition of certain fundamental skills because the child is just too passive to acquire them. On the other hand, hyperactivity interferes with the acquisition of certain fundamental skills because the child cannot concentrate on any one task long enough to learn the skills. This may be true. But some people go further and suggest that hyperactivity and hyperpassivity are masculine and feminine qualities, respectively. This is untrue. They are exaggerations of normal gender roles. Hence the next step of the argument, that unmitigated masculinity and femininity are harmful, becomes suspect. Certainly, exaggeration of a role seems harmful, but very few individuals are ever at such extremes.

Other research tries to show how androgyny (defined

as a balance of masculinity and femininity) is indicative of optimal functioning. The leader of this research effort is Sandra Bem at Stanford University. I should like to discuss some of her research findings. Typically, she administers her BSRI to university students and then categorizes each student into one of several groups, depending on the score he or she obtains on the BSRI. She usually sets up three groups for further examination. These groups are composed of those who are (1) significantly sex typed, (2) significantly sex reversed, and (3) androgynous.

In the first study (Bem 1975), she asked individuals to rate various cartoons for their funniness. The room was set up so as to make the individual believe there were actually a number of people rating these cartoons, each in a separate booth, but with a common intercom system. In fact, the other voices the individual heard were from a tape played over the intercom system. On a number of trials, the voices gave "false replies" suggesting that a cartoon was funny when it was not, or that it was not funny when it actually was.

She found, as she expected, that masculine individuals (irrespective of their biological sex) did not conform to false reports of funniness. They said that funny cartoons were funny and that unhumorous cartoons were not funny. This, Bem said, was a sign of independence, which is a masculine trait. She also found that, in comparison to the behavior of masculine individuals, feminine individuals conformed more to the false reports. This conformity was judged to be a feminine trait, so that this finding was also not surprising. The interesting result was that androgynous individuals tended to be more like masculine than feminine individuals. They were relatively independent.

Bem implicitly placed a positive value on independence and a negative value on conformity in this study. She suggested that her results showed behavioral rigidity in the feminine group; however, the feminine group's rigidity is neither more nor less than the rigidity of the masculine and the androgynous groups. Where the feminine group displays "rigid" conformity, the masculine and androgynous groups display a "rigid" independence. And the task of rating the funniness of cartoons is so unimportant as to preclude discussion of which response is better in this situation.

There is an equally plausible explanation of the results that places a negative value on independence. Many of the individuals involved in the study had learned about tests of conformity. Bem knew of some of these individuals and excluded their scores from the results. But what of the others? Imagine yourself in the situation. You are helping a psychologist with her study. You think several others are also helping, but unfortunately their sense of humor is not very keen. Do you *impulsively assert* yourself and say that the others' conception of funniness is different from yours; or do you *reflect* on the situation and surmise that by asserting yourself you may jeopardize the study? If the latter, you may decide to be helpful and yield to others' opinions. Let me give a better example of how conformity may be a good trait. Miss Jones buys a new dress that looks atrocious. You can tell her the truth and hurt her feelings. Or, you can conform to what everyone else is doing and tell her it looks nice.

Next, Bem had a series of students play with a kitten. She then placed each student in a room containing the kitten and other objects. It was noted how involved the student became with the kitten as opposed to the other objects.

This time the results were not as clear-cut. Feminine males, as expected, displayed more feminine "nurturance" (i.e. played with the kitten more) than did masculine males. Androgynous males also displayed feminine nurturance. However, of all three groups, the feminine females displayed the *least* so-called feminine nurturance. This result would seriously undermine the assumption that playing with a kitten is a feminine activity. At any rate, Bem did show that androgynous females display higher levels of nurturance than feminine females.

In a third study, students were told that the experimenter was preparing to do a study concerning a person's attribution of another's personality as affected by the particular activity in which the other is engaged. For this, she explained, she needed pictures of the student engaged in various activities, which pictures she would then use in her study of personality attribution. In fact, none of this was true but was a diversion to keep the students from guessing the true purpose of the study.

Various activities were arranged in pairs, and each student was asked to select the one activity from each pair that he would prefer to perform when his picture was taken. In addition, the student received a few pennies for each choice, with some choices paying more than others.

Of the thirty pairs of activities presented to each individual, five consisted of a male activity (e.g. nailing boards) and a female activity (e.g. ironing cloth napkins); five consisted of a male activity and a neutral activity (e.g. playing with a Yo-Yo); and five consisted of a female activity and a neutral activity. In each pair, the less gender-appropriate activity paid more.

Bem found that sex-typed individuals—masculine males and feminine females—were significantly more stereotyped in their choices than were androgynous or sex-reversed individuals, which two groups were not different from one another. Bem believed this was the proof she needed. Sex-typed individuals were more rigid in their preference of activities, even to the point that they received less money than those who would choose opposite-sex activities.

So Bem, who has done more than the three studies discussed above, has adequately demonstrated that one's gender role adoption as assessed by her test is associated with one's gender role adoption as per behavioral indices. She has also shown that the androgynous individual, in any test situation, tends to adopt the typical response of one sex or the other. But herein, I feel, lies a dilemma that Bem has not explicitly dealt with in her writings.

She defines androgyny as a balance between

masculinity and femininity. If this is so, then in any situation involving a gender role discrimination, an androgynous person should sometimes respond as would a masculine individual and sometimes as would a feminine individual. For example, in a room containing a kitten and a three-dimensional maze (a masculine plaything). a feminine individual should play with the kitten, a masculine individual should play with the maze, and an androgynous individual *should* split his time between the two. But the persons defined as androgynous do not display masculine and feminine traits equally in such a situation. Why? This seems beyond any reasonable explanation except the possibility of experimental bias.

Experimental bias is the phenomenon whereby the experimenter's beliefs about what should occur in the experiment are transmitted to the experimental subject, with the result that the subject responds according to the experimenter's beliefs. This is a very subtle process. When the androgynous or feminine individuals were left alone with the kitten and the maze, there might have been an intonation or slight emphasis on the word *kitten* or a fleeting glance toward the kitten. When masculine individuals were tested, the experimenter could have subtly highlighted the word *maze* or glanced toward the maze. This is speculation, but it is indeed a possibility—especially since Bem self-admittedly feels a personal and emotional commitment to her hypothesis about androgyny. Otherwise, it just does not make sense that a person with both male and female qualities should respond to a gender-related testing situation with only male or only female qualitites—depending on which Bem feels is more indicative of mental health in that particular situation. Androgynous persons should display male and female qualities equally. But they do not. Something is amiss.

Another aspect of Bem's studies that concerns me is the possibility of reactive effects of the measuring instrument, the BSRI. As was previously noted, the students first completed the BSRI and then, at a later date, participated in the rest of the study. The fact is that a student might remember giving himself high masculinity ratings and, in order to preserve his integrity, chose to have his picture taken nailing boards rather than ironing napkins. The possible reactive effects of the measuring instrument should not be lightly dismissed. It takes a more complicated experimental design than the one she is using to account for such effects.

Finally, even if there were no such problems with Bem's studies, the results are, at best, a demonstration that behavior is often dependent, not on an individual's biological sex, but on his psychological sex; and that the androgynous individual exhibits behavior appropriate for either a masculine or a feminine person, but not both. From this, Bem deduces that it is psychologically advantageous to be androgynous. She hopes that one day androgyny can define a new standard of mental health.

But look at the data presented in Chapter IV. Psychiatric inpatients and outpatients tend to be more androgynous than their nonpatient peers. What type of mental health is this? Are those requiring psychiatric assistance to be our new norm of mental health? Bem's studies are interesting, but she attempts too broad a leap from her studies of behavior and personality to conclusions about mental health.

In fact, her thesis that androgynous individuals are more behaviorally flexible than other people has met head-on with Heilbrun's (1976) data that indicate androgynous individuals are more behaviorally rigid. That is, these two researchers have reported conflicting evidence. This is nothing surprising in the field of psychology. What is surprising is the fact that both Heilbrun and Bem are apparent supporters of androgyny—to the point that Bem defines behavioral flexibility as mentally *healthy* (because her androgynous individuals seemed flexible), and Heilbrun defines behavioral flexibility as mentally *unhealthy* (because his androgynous individuals seemed less flexible than masculine or feminine individuals).

Obviously we are caught in the midst of a very emotionally laden area. People are trying to support causes, and data are pouring out faster than researchers can plan good studies. In fact, data are being amassed before individuals are even sure what they are trying to prove—other than "androgyny is good." We must step back and critically evaluate the output of information. Being androgynous means something, and that meaning may be different from either masculinity or femininity. But at present it is certain that androgyny cannot be said to mean mental health. In fact, evidence points to its meaning mental maladjustment. But more work is needed.

For certain, people should not try, at this point, to raise androgynous children. It would be a premature move. Possibly the androgynous upbringing would actually be harmful to the child. Our society is still largely sex typed, and expects its individuals to have a moderate amount of sex typing. The individual who does not is seen as deviant and labeled as such. Society may reject him.

The line between androgyny and undifferentiation may be a tenuous one. As you may recall, androgyny has recently been defined as the possession of both masculine and feminine traits to a marked degree. Undifferentiation, on the other, is defined as the possession of few markedly masculine or feminine traits. The attempt to raise a child whose masculinity is in equal balance with his femininity may result in a child who is so confused he learns neither masculinity nor femininity, but becomes an undifferentiated individual—which is, presumably, the worst possible outcome.

Remember, we are dealing with young children. Their sex is a cornerstone to a self-definition, and their sexual identity is essential for personality development. Even those who favor androgyny, which applies only to gender role, acknowledge the importance of a stable and well-defined gender identity. Attempts to train a very young child might influence, not only his gender role, but also his gender identity.

This is particularly true in our sex-typed society. The

child raised to display both masculine and feminine traits may begin to redefine his basic identity when he notices how different he is from sex-typed individuals. He may say to himself, "I like to fight, and I like to dress dolls. What am I? Am I a boy or a girl?"

If our entire society were androgynous, we might want to foster androgyny in our children. But in a sex-typed society, children brought up to be androgynous are like storm troops on a beachhead. They form the first wave in a hostile environment. As with all storm troops, there will be a high rate of casualties among them. And we are not even sure that the beachhead is worth it.

Further, to be truly androgynous may be beyond the capability of children. Parents know how difficult it is to teach a child almost anything. It is difficult to teach a boy to play baseball and to teach a girl how to make doll clothes. Imagine the difficulty in teaching a child everything you would teach either sex. Again, there is something to the idea of specialization. Teach a person the decathlon, and he just cannot do as well at all events as would specialists in those events.

Also to be considered is that androgyny does not involve high masculinity and high femininity at the same time. Androgyny is the ability to display high masculinity or high femininity in various situations, depending on which is more appropriate. That is, a truly androgynous individual should be assertive and dominant if he is shortchanged in a restaurant, but should be yielding and submissive if he has run into the back of a police car. So to teach androgyny to a child not only requires teaching him twice as much, but also implies teaching him to differentiate in what situations to use which set of traits.

It is so much more economical and feasible to teach either masculinity or femininity. Let a little boy be assertive across all situations. He will learn in which situations he should inhibit his assertiveness. This discrimination is much easier than also having to decide whether to display some feminine trait in a situation in which a masculine trait should be inhibited.

Discrimination and differentiation, in terms both of

the existence of two sexes and of the individual's self-designation as a member of one sex, is of utmost importance for psychological health. In our sex-typed society, an androgynous individual may be impaired in his ability to differentiate which of two sets of roles he should adopt. Some classic animal studies have shown that an inability to differentiate between two simple categories can lead to symptoms resembling human neurosis. I suggest that psychiatric patients and clients, who are less sex-typed than most people, have developed their psychological problems as a result of their inability to adopt a single gender role. They are essentially lost, do not have the ability to differentiate, and subsequently develop psychopathological symptoms. An androgynous society would *decrease* male/female differences, making differentiation more difficult for the child. As differentiation became harder, the incidence of psychopathological symptoms would increase. An androgynous society would create more mental health problems than it would solve.

Our society, sex typed as it is, is just not ready for androgyny. We would do our children an injustice to try to forge them into an androgynous mold. It does sound good on paper: a child with both sets of traits should have advantages over one with only one set of traits. But in actual practice, such a child is put at a disadvantage.

At this point I should like to make clear that, to me, a sex-typed society is not synonymous with a sexist society. A sex-typed society is one in which male and female roles are distinct. A sexist society is one in which one sex suffers discrimination. Our society is not only sex typed, but it is also sexist, despite legislation. My own belief is that there is something good about a sex-typed society. I know of no society that is not, somehow, sex typed. I think this condition provides a certain stability to life. It lays down certain ways that males and females are to be different. This provides an individual with some yardstick with which to measure himself. It gives people, especially children, certain goals for which to strive. It clearly defines, using biological sex as the landmark, the different paths that one should follow.

Sexism, on the other hand, is bad. It produces conflict between the two sexes, and such conflict actually can work against some of the benefits of sex typing. Sexism also leads individuals to erroneously attack sex typing. Many who are involved in the fight against sexism take a dim view of sex typing. I was once berated by a female who was obviously sensitive to the problem of sexism. She claimed one of my studies was *unscientific* because I was testing males and females and, therefore, looking for a sex difference. A study cannot be unscientific for this reason. But she felt strongly about sexism and decided to attack sex-typing as something she saw as similar to sexism.

But sex typing need not play any role in sexism, or vice versa. Even if males and females were identical in their psychological makeup and biological abilities, there would still exist two sexes, and sexism would remain possible. Even if the only difference between male and female were that one possessed a penis and the other a vagina, sexism could still exist. If the color of one's skin can lead to discrimination, certainly the configuration of one's genitals can, too.

Therefore, while I cannot endorse androgyny, and even advise against it at this point in time, I am not endorsing sexism either. I believe the sexes are different and that they should be different. But I also believe that one sex should not be discriminated against because of any of these differences.

Summary

There has recently been a move toward a less sex-divided society. Such a society, wherein differences between males and females are negligible, is known as androgynous. Some researchers have suggested that androgyny is beneficial to mental health. However, studies with psychologically maladjusted groups seem to contradict that belief. Students seeking professional assistance for mental health problems are more androgynous than are more well-adjusted students. Also, male psychiatric patients are more androgynous than nonpatients. So, if anything, androgyny is hazardous for mental health. The reason may be that an androgynous individual is out of place in our sex-typed society. As such, he may be viewed as deviant. Further, an androgynous upbringing or an androgynous identity deprives the individual of that one important self-defining characteristic: a definite sexual identity.

XI.
Summary and Future Directives

The previous chapters have dealt with defining and measuring sexual identity, the development of sexual identity, some of the problems that can occur when sexual identity is not developed properly, and some institutions in our society that may exert a feminizing or masculinizing influence. This chapter is concerned with what we can and should do about some of the problems discussed in the preceding chapters.

We have seen that sexual identity is important, particularly for the male, in order to develop a mature and psychologically healthy personality. A problem associated with sexual identity formation may result in a faulty personality development and in psychological maladjustment. Problems in sexual identity formation may also lead to sexual variations. While many of these variations are more indicative of social maladjustment than of psychological maladjustment, they can act as a source

of pressure on the individual and may produce psychological distress.

The first and most important goal, then, to to help
the child develop a secure and defined gender identity, or
sense of belonging to one biological sex. This is a point
almost no one would debate. It is good for a child to have
this sense of belonging to one of the sexes. It is one grip
on reality. It is one part in the overallall puzzle of self-definition. It is an important cornerstone upon which the
child can build.

Since gender identity is crystallized around eighteen
months of age, it is essential that the proper atmosphere
exist in the child's earliest months. In Chapter II, we discussed some conditions that may be conducive to the development of a proper gender identity. The most important consideration is a proper body image. An
individual gains his body image chiefly through self-ex-
plorations. The infant often plays with his various body
parts. When he does so, he receives feedback. If he bites
his toes, he feels the bite. He learns that those wiggly
little things are a part of him. He learns to discriminate
the location of different sensations. He learns that different parts of his body feel different to the touch, and that
touching different parts provides different sensations.

He also learns from the stimulation others pro-vide
for his body. When parents play with different parts of
the child's body (e.g. mock fighting with arms, or mock
walking with the legs), the child learns about these different parts through body feedback.

Mirror behavior, which begins around seven months
of age, also helps the child acquire a body image. He
learns that the figure in the mirror is himself. The mirror
allows him perspectives of himself, and views of certain
body parts that would be unattainable otherwise.

We have also seen that discrimination between male
and female helps a child establish his gender identity. If
an individual thought there were just one body type for
everyone, he could not sex-type himself. It is important

that he learn the physical basis for such discrimination. If he does not know that a male has a penis and a female a vagina, the child, even if aware of his own body image, may fail to develop a sense of belonging to one sex or the other. He runs the risk of developing a sense of belonging to the opposite sex. That is, for the development of a proper sexual identity, the child must not only develop a proper body image but must also know to which of two camps his body type belongs.

Some of the factors that contribute to such knowledge were previously discussed. One of the most common is the presence of opposite-sex siblings. A brother or sister is, in many cases, the first person of the opposite sex that an individual can remember seeing in the nude. Parental nudity also provides a chance for the child to learn to anatomically discriminate the sexes. In some cases, pictures of nude males and females may be available to the child.

Sex discrimination, and to a large extent the development of gender identity, is a function of language acquisition. Parents and significant others give numerous verbal clues as to the child's sex and to the fact that there are two sexes. "What a nice little boy . . . Daddy's little girl . . . Nice little girls don't do that . . . Well, he's certainly a tough little boy" are all statements that tell the child, "You are a boy" or "You are a girl." Such verbal statements also tell the child that there are two sexes. A male child is told, "You're a tough little man." But his sister is told, "You're such a sweet little lady." He also learns that the words *boy* or *man* are used for individuals with certain noticeable differences from the individuals tagged as *girls* or *women*. For example, men have shorter hair and never wear dresses; women never have moustaches but do have breasts. The distinction based on genitals is much less obvious to a child who never sees people nude. Hence, for a child not exposed to nudity, language becomes of paramount importance for the development of gender identity.

So what does this mean for parents? Are there schedules they can follow to make sure they are doing things properly? Can they, or should they, hasten this process of gender identity formation? Are they doing anything that might jeopardize an appropriate gender identity formation? Probably the best thing concerned parents can do is not to become overly concerned. They should especially avoid communicating such a concern to the child. To him, the communication might read, "I'm so afraid that you are not really a boy/girl."

Most parents seem to consciously or unconsciously treat the sexes differently and in a way conducive to appropriate gender identity development. Rather than monitor their own behavior to make sure they are doing the right things, parents would do better to make sure they are not doing the wrong things.

Overpossessiveness, overprotection, overcloseness to the child, particularly by the parent of the opposite sex, may inhibit the child's sense of uniqueness or his sense of separateness from that parent. A sense of separateness from the opposite-sex parent is crucial in the development of an appropriate gender identity. A close bond between a mother and a male child, for example, confuses the child by making him feel as if he is one with the mother (and therefore a part of a female) as well as male (which he is).

Another problem area is an overly puritanical attitude on the part of parents. Such an attitude could inhibit either the child's self-exploration or the presentation of nudity, and squelch a child's body image development as a result. If a child is constantly punished for examining his genitals or for touching taboo body areas, the body image may be impaired at the point where its development is most essential. Further, an overly strict attitude dealing with the genitals may lead the child to believe that the genitals themselves are evil. Such an attitude could lead him to believe that it would have been better to have been born without genitals or with a different set of genitals. The child who is punished for playing with his penis may think he is being punished because he possesses a penis. He may think, "If I did not have a penis, my mother would not punish me." And punishment and dislike are often equated by the child. Hence, to gain his mother's love, now translated as lack of punishment, he may wish that he had no penis, which wish might later be transformed to regret having been born a male.

An obsession with avoiding nudity also inhibits the child's ability to discriminate on the basis of anatomy. It not only precludes a knowledge of the foundations upon which sex categorization is made, but also prevents him from placing himself into one of the cagegories on the basis of his own anatomical features. This places a heavy burden on language and verbal clues for the development of a proper gender identity.

Needless to say, verbal clues given to a child should be appropriate and clear. Repeatedly telling a girl that she is a boy will likely result in a masculine or, at least, confused gender identity. This would be true even if the girl had developed a proper body image and sex-discrimination ability. As noted in Chapter II, individuals whose anatomy was contrary to their assigned sex, with its concomitant verbal clues, developed a sexual identity appropriate to their assigned sex.

The development of a stable and appropriate gender identity is an important and basic step. But other steps follow. With regard to gender role there is a debate whether androgyny is best, appropriate sex typing is best, or masculinity is best. For males, at least, I am convinced that appropriate sex typing is most conducive to mental health.

From the extended discussion presented in Chapter II, one should be able to detect some of the measures that can lead a child into gender role behavior. There are two basic steps to this process. One is modelling the behavior, and the other is reinforcing it.

Studies have shown that a child's initial learning of

various behaviors is based upon, or at least facilitated by, the imitation of a person who serves as a model. Modeling seems to put the individual in the state where he knows the behavior and is prepared, within the limits of his abilities, to display that behavior himself. Therefore, if you want your child go grow up asssertive, let him see someone who is assertive. If you wish your child to grow up neat and tidy, he should first have models who are neat and tidy.

Even though a child may try out a behavior on the basis of modelling alone, whether or not he continues that behavior depends on reinforcement. If a person is praised for some behavior or given a reward of some other kind, the chances are that the behavior will recur. If a behavior elicits no response from anyone, the chances are that the behavior will discontinue; punishment tends to decrease a behavior. But it has two possible disadvantages. One is that punishment may actually be a source of reinforcement. A child may resort to disapproved behavior because he knows it will get him immediate attention. The other problem is that punishment in one situation, such as at home, decreases the behavior in that situation; but it might not decrease the behavior in other situations, such as at school.

To illustrate the consequences of reinforcement, suppose a boy sees his father hammering nails (modeling). The child now has that behavior in his mind as something he himself might do. If the child does begin hammering his father could reinforce him by saying, "Wow, you're helping daddy. Thanks." The behavior will probably continue. But if the father ignores the behavior, it will probably discontinue.

"Time and again," a parent may complain, "I've punished Johnny for running down the stairs, but he still does it." Punishment of a behavior is *not* the same as ignoring a behavior, but could actually act as a reinforcement. Johnny may want the parent's attention so much that he does not care whether the attention is approving or disapproving. The unfortunate fact of much of life is that bad deed receive more attention than good deeds do. Or, as Shakespeare had Marc Antony say in *Julius Caesar*, "The evil that men do lives after them, the good is oft' interred with their bones."

Another problem is that parents often give conflicting messages to the child. For example, after Johnny uses the hammer, daddy says, "How nice that Johnny is helping daddy." But then Johnny may try to hammer when daddy is not in such a good mood, when daddy is sleeping or when daddy has a hangover. Obviously, under these conditions, hammering will not be given the social approval it once received. But once the behavior has been reinforced, it may continue and may even increase in frequency, even if daddy manages to ignore it subsequently.

This is a firmly established finding in animal research. If an animal is given several reinforcements for some behavior and reinforcement is then discontinued, the behavior increases in frequency and continues for a long time despite the lack of reinforcement. Also, intermittent reinforcement—for example, reinforcement every twenty-fifth time a behavior is exhibited—leads to the most consistent and highest levels of behavioral enactment. So telling Johnny a few times that he is a good boy for hammering, ignoring his hammering behavior for a week, then once again saying that it is nice that he is helping daddy hammer, leads to more hammering behavior than telling Johnny every day that he is a good boy for helping daddy hammer.

One can now see that even a few reinforcements of behavior may lead to a display of that behavior—even if it is subsequently punished or ignored. It is easier to prevent a behavior from developing than to stop it once it has been reinforced.

Children often take on opposite-sex behaviors, clothes, or games. Childhood is a time when people experiment with various alternatives to see how each feels.

When this happens, it would probably be best if the parents do not make a fuss over it, in either a positive or a negative way. If the behavior is lightly dismissed, the chances are that the child will discontinue it and try something else that might obtain some reinforcement for him. However, if such cross-sexed behavior continues, it should no longer be ignored. Parents or professionals should intervene to guide the child into a more appropriate pattern of behavior.

Let me stress that the worst thing a parent can do is become overly concerned about the child's masculinity or femininity. Most children develop rather normally. But if there are noticeable problems in the child's development, parents should look to themselves. They should make sure they are not in some way jeopardizing the child's sexual identity. The few situations previously mentioned as "do nots" should be seriously considered by parents of infants. Much of a child's later development is determined by the path he takes in his first eighteen months of life. These are crucial months for sexual identity development.

I would also urge parents not to bring up an androgynous or unisex child at this time. Sufficient data have not been collected to show that this type of development is beneficial. In fact, the parent may do the child a grave disservice.

As noted in Chapter 6, the elementary school is a feminized atmosphere that works against boys and for girls. A number of reccommendations for change are apparent.

First, the overwhelming preponderance of female teachers and male administrators should be changed. Most of the principals and other administrators were once teachers themselves. Possibly we should not be so quick to give males the administrative positions. If women got more of the promotions, more men could interact with the children. Obviously, this proposition will not sit well with male administrators and aspiring male administrators, since principals have more prestige and higher salaries than classroom teachers.

However, there are other alternatives. One is to require principals and vice-principals to take one class period a week for each class. This would leave less time for administrative chores, but hiring a female assistant sould solve that problem. This plan would allow all the children to see an adult male authority, and to see him at times other than when they have done something wrong. Or, if there are a few male teachers in the school, they could switch a few class periods with the female teachers so that all the students have both male and female teachers. A final suggestion is to ask for male volunteers from the community to come into the school and interact with the children. They could join the children for lunches, supervise their play periods, or even serve as teachers' assistants.

More male teachers should be enlisted, not only because they add a male element to an all-female environment, but also because students with male teachers seem to fare better than students with female teachers. Male teachers, or more males about the school, would also make the transition into the masculine environment of high school and college a smoother occurence.

More time should be devoted to such male activities as gym and science. A more serious attitude toward male activity such as gym would help the boy feel that it is good he can do well at this. Gym is presently treated too much like a game. "So what if he's good at gym—it's not a serious subject," many people think. Such attitudes need to be changed.

Teachers should be made aware of the difference between a boy who lacks academic talent and one who does poorly academically because of "behavioral problems." And teachers should also know that many "behavioral problems" are no more than typical boyish behavior. True, a certain amount of discipline is necessary to run a class. True, boys cause most of the disciplinary problems. But their behavior and their academic ability should be judged separately. Teachers should be more concerned with their "teacher's pet" male, who has not adopted a male gender role, than with their discipline-problem males. The boys who present extreme disciplinary or behavioral problems might best be referred for professional help.

Female teachers should become sensitive to the reinforcement they give their students. They should be wary of reinforcing feminine behavior in both male and female pupils. Gym and recess would be excellent times to give the boys positive reinforcement for masculine behavior.

The problems of masculinized higher education are tougher to solve. Unlike the elementary school, where the minority of teachers, the males, form the majority of administrators, universities have relatively few females in either teaching or administrative positions. So it would not help to ask administrators to take over more teaching responsibilities. Also, the higher degree of training necessary for university teaching precludes bringing in females from the community to act as assistants.

The main area available for change seems to be the competitive atmosphere. Several alternative methods of easing competition have been proposed. One is to let students grade themselves. I have been involved in several attempts at this alternative and, have found too many students who take advantage of it. True, some do work and some earn the grade they give themselves, but many see it as an easy grade. This is not a feasible alternative unless some group of limits, guidelines, or rules is also imposed.

I have also let students work in groups and receive one group grade. This was to ensure that group members work for and with each other. Also, each group was to be judged purely on its merits and not in comparison with other groups. In fact, the delineation of meritorious work was harder than one might think, and groups *were* compared with one another. And in one group, contrary to my hope of group cohesion, a fraction of the workers split themselves off from the rest of the group and handed in a separate project *because* they felt that their work was better than the work done by the rest of the group. So, even though the teacher tried to avoid competitiveness, the students had been so well trained and so immersed in it that they themselves could not avoid competition.

I have even heard of situations where a teacher was willing to let the class members draw straws for their grades, but the students themselves refused. They were afraid that one wrong draw could cost them a place in graduate school or a fellowship. It seems that the competitive nature of higher education is learned early and is extremely resistant to change.

Even females, and in some cases particularly females, get caught up in this competitive atmosphere, even though they seem to suffer the most from it. They, too, take advantage of self-grading, prefer not to draw straws, and are loathe to work in groups for group grades.

The competitiveness and masculinized atmosphere of the university is hard to kill. So much rides on a student's grades. Perhaps there would be less competition if grades were done away with and a student received either a pass or a not pass for each subject. In fact, some schools have tried this system. Most of the competition results from trying to be "on top" with an A or B grade. With pass-fail grading, there is no "top." All but a very few nonworkers receive a pass. Students in such a system might compete less against one another, might help their fellow students more, might be less agentic and more communal. Females might do better, psychologically, in this type of system.

With regard to future directives for the psychiatric institution, it seems essential that male staff spend more time on the wards. More females should be put into administrative positions. Or men should share administrative duties with the women so that the men have more time for patient contact. Increased interaction between male staff and male patients seems necessary.

Possibly a structured athletic period could be worked into the schedule to counteract the feminizing effects of group meetings, art therapy, television watching, and card playing. Give the male patient a time in which he can properly vent his masculinity. He needs to be assertive and aggressive and not be punished for it.

Some sort of gender role training in the hospital would also help. Assertion training, especially for the males, should become a ward activity. More manly magazines, to replace a few of the neutral and feminine magazines, might be of value. Treating the patients more as individual males and females rather than as patients per se might reinforce appropriate sexual identity feelings.

The male patient should be encouraged to be self-sufficient and self-reliant. He should not be told that the hospital will take care of all his needs. He should be stimulated and motivated to take care of himself and to get back out as soon as possible.

In one rather daring move, a small group of male and female schizophrenic patients was encouraged to engage in sexual activity with one another. Improvement in symptomatology was apparent after such supportive heterosexual experiences (Nell 1968). The heterosexual encounters certainly provided encouragement and reinforcement of the patients' sexual identity. While such daring may not be anticipated as ward routine in the near future, it does seem apparent that treating patients more like individuals and allowing for differences according to biological sex facilitates recovery.

In the distant future, such techniques may cease to raise eyebrows. Certainly, most people disapproved when in the late 1700s the French physician Pinel unchained mental patients, brought them out into the community, and treated them humanely. But today, placing the patient in the community as soon as possible is a common occurrence.

Finally, the psychotherapy relationship should take into consideration the sex differences that make therapy more difficult for males than for females.

One hope is the role induction or anticipatory socialization interview. Before actual therapy begins, the client is made aware of the roles he and the therapist will take on in therapy itself. The person learns that it is essential to be expressive, honest, verbal, and so forth. This approach has been shown to reduce strain in the relationship and has been associated with a better therapy outcome.

But even with role induction, females do better than males in psychotherapy. This is probably because the female has had more practice with the required role. Even though a role induction interview prepares the male for the role he is to take on, he may still be less able than the female to carry out that role, which for him is a temporarily adopted one. However, the role induction probably gives him some assurance that this is how therapy works and that he will act in a feminine manner in order to make it work, not because he is feminine. The female role adoption does not reflect on his masculinity, since it is clear that feminine traits are temporarily adopted for the therapy session and are not a part of his nature.

Precisely because the role requirements are not part of his nature, we may wish to give the male a little extra edge. This we could do by coaching or training in the anticipated role. The use of other males to model appropriate psychotherapy behavior may be helpful. If some of these ideas are implemented, the male may benefit as much from psychotherapy as does the female.

The male's reluctance to enter psychotherapy because he sees it as a feminine alternative is another problem that must be solved. But such reluctance is difficult to overcome, since it is linked with the male role of

being self-sufficient and self-reliant. Perhaps we may
wish to temper, not change, this role behavior. It would
be better if males, too, were encouraged to seek help when
help is necessary. Perhaps the community mental health
movement will remove some of the stigma associated
with psychiatric aid. Community workers might be able
to seek out troubled individuals instead of waiting for the
troubled person to seek out aid himself.

The therapist himself should be sensitized to this
problem area for the male. He could step out of role just a
little for the male client and take over more of the verbal
responsibility, or even model some of the desired behavior, in a few of the initial sessions. If nothing else, this
problem area could be brought up in a psychotherapy
session and discussed as an area of strain for the client.

Conclusion

Presented in this chapter have been a few
suggestions which, if implemented, might avoid some
problems related to the sexual identity of individuals.
Some of these problems concern development of sexual
identity. But even after sexual identity has been formed,
it can crash head-on with institutions or settings that
work against it.

Ideally, we would all be sensitized to how our behavior can cause problems for others' sexual identities, and
we would be aware of the impact of our own sexual
identity in our daily life activities. Sexual identity is important for each individual. Society should not only
provide different equipment for the two sexes (e.g.
bathrooms, clothing styles), it should also provide for different sexual identities. This may never happen, but if it
did, we might all live happily ever after.

References

Adler, A. 1956. *The individual psychology of Alfred Adler.* Eds. H. L. Ansbacher and R. R, Ansbacher. New York: Basic Books.

Adler, A. 1964. *The practice and theory of individual psychology.* Translated by P. Radin. London: Routledge & Kegan Paul.

Apfeldorf, M., and Smith, W. J. 1966. The representation of the body self in human figure drawings. *Journal of Projective Techniques* 30:467-70.

Arnold, R. D. 1968. The achievement of boys and girls taught by men and women teachers. *Elementary School Journal* 68:367-72.

Bakan, D. 1966. *The duality of human existence.* Chicago: Rand McNally.

Bakwin, H., and Bakwin, R. 1966. *Clinical manifestations of behavior disorders in children.* New York: Saunders.

Bem, S. 1974. The psychological measurement of androgyny. *Journal of Consulting & Clinical Psychology* 42:155-62.

Bem, S. 1975. Beyond androgyny: Some presumptuous prescriptions for a liberated sexual identity. Paper presented at the APA-NIMH Conference on the Research Needs of Women, 31 May, 1975, Madison, Wis.

Biller, H. B. 1973. Paternal and sex-role factors in cognitive and academic functioning. In *Nebraska symposium on motivation*, ed. J. K. Cole and R. Dienstbier, 21:83-123. Lincoln: University of Nebraska Press.

Block, J. H. 1973. Conceptions of sex role. Some cross-cultural and longitudinal perspectives. *American Psychologist* 28:512-26.

Caudill, W. 1958. *The psychiatric hospital as a small society.* Cambridge, Mass.: Harvard University Press.

Cozby, P. C. 1973. Self-disclosure: A literature review. *Psychological Bulletin* 79:73-91.

Fagot, B. I., and Patterson, G. R. 1969. An in vivo analysis of reinforcing contingencies in the preschool child. *Developmental Psychology* 1:563-68.

Fisk, N. 1973. Gender dysphoria syndrome. (The how, what, and why of a disease). In *Proceedings of the second interdisciplinary symposium on gender dysphoria syndrome*, ed. D. R. Laub and P. Gandy, pp. 7-14. Stanford, Calif.: Stanford University Medical Center.

Franck, K., and Rosen, E. 1949. A projective test of masculinity-femininity. *Journal of Consulting Psychology* 13:247-56.

Freud, S. 1925. Psycho-analytic notes upon an autobiographical account of a case of paranoia (dementia paranoides). In *Collected Papers*, 3:390-472. Edinburgh, Great Britain: R. & R. Clark.

Gershman, H. 1970. The role of core gender identity in the genesis of perversions. *American Journal of Psychoanalysis* 30:58-67.

Green, R. 1974. *Sexual identity conflict in children and adults.* New York: Basic Books.

Hampson, J. L., and Hampson, J. G. 1961. The ontogenesis of sexual behavior in man. In *Sex and internal secretions*, ed. W. C. Young, 3rd edit., 2:1407-32.

Hanson, E. H. 1959. Do boys get a square deal in school? *Education* 79:597-98.

Heilbrun, A. B., Jr. 1973. Parent identification and filial sex-role behavior: The importance of biological context. In *Nebraska symposium on motivation*, ed. J. K. Cole and R. Dienstbier, 21:125-94. Lincoln: University of Nebraska Press.

Heilbrun, A. B., Jr. 1976. Measurement of masculine and feminine sex role identities as independent dimensions. *Journal of Consulting and Clinical Psychology* 44:183-90.

Howard, K. I. and Orlinsky, D. E. 1972. Psychotherapeutic process. *Annual Review of Psychology* 23:615-68.

Kleeman, J. A. 1971. The establishment of core gender identity in normal girls. II. How meanings are conveyed between parent and child in the first three years. *Archives of Sexual Behavior* 1:117-29.

Krafft-Ebing, R. von 1933. *Paychopathia sexualis.* New York: Physicians and Surgeons Book Co.

LaTorre, R. A. 1975. Gender and age as factors in the attitudes toward those stigmatized as mentally ill. *Journal of Consulting and Clinical Psychology* 43:97-98.

LaTorre, R. A. 1976. The psychological assessment off gender identity and gender role in schizophrenia. *Schizophrenia Bulletin* 2:266-85.

LaTorre, R. A. 1978. Gender role and psychological adjustment. *Archives of Sexual Behavior* 7:89-96.

LaTorre, R. A., Endman, M., and Gossmann, I. 1976. Androgyny and need achievement in male and female psychiatric inpatients. *Journal of Clinical Psychology* 32:233-35.

LaTorre, R. A., Gossmann, I., and Piper, W. E. 1976. Cognitive style, hemispheric specialization, and tested abilities of transsexuals and nontranssexuals. *Perceptual and Motor Skills* 43:719-22.

LaTorre, R. A., and Grégoire, P. A. 1977. Gender role in university health clients. *Journal of Inidividual Psychology*, 33:246-49.

LaTorre, R. A., and Piper, W. E. 1978. The Terman-Miles M-F Test: An examination of exercises 1, 2, and 3 forty years later. *Sex Roles*, 4:141-54.

Lester, D. 1975. The relationship between paranoid delusions and homosexuality. *Archives of Sexual Behavior* 4:285-94.

Lewis, M. 1972. There's no unisex in the nursery. *Psychology Today*, May 1972, 54-57.

Lidz, T. 1972. The nature and origins of schizophrenic disorders. *Annals of Internal Medicine* 77:639-45.

May, R. 1970. Paranoia and power anxiety. *Journal of Projective Techniques* 34:412-18.

McClelland, D. C. 1961. *The achieving society*. Princeton, N. J.: Van Nostrand.

Money, J., and Ehrhardt, A. A. 1968. *Man & Woman, Boy & Girl*. Baltimore: John Hopkins University Press.

Nell, R. 1968. Sex in a mental institution. *Journal of Sex Research* 4:303-12.

Page, J., and Warkentin, J. 1938. Masculinity and paranoia. *Journal of Abnormal and Social Psychology* 33:527-31.

Paitich, D. 1973. Psychological test assessment of gender patients. In *Proceedings of the second interdisciplinary symposium on gender dysphoria syndrome*, ed. D. R. Laub and P. Gandy, pp. 96-98. Stanford, Calif.: Stanford University Medical Center.

Parsons, T., and Bales, R. F. 1953. *Family, socialization and interaction process*. Glencoe, Ill.: Free Press.

Reuter, M. W., and Biller, H. B. 1973. Perceived paternal nurturance-availability and personality adjustment among college males. *Journal of Consulting and Clinical Psychology* 40:339.

Schatzberg, A. F., Westfall, M. P., Blumetti, A. B., and Birk, C. L. 1975. Effeminacy. I. A quantitative rating scale. *Archives of Sexual Behavior* 4:31-41.

Schell, R. E., and Silber, J. W. 1968. Sex-role discrimination among young children. *Perceptual and Motor Skills* 27:379-89.

Seyfried, B. A., and Hendrick, C. 1973. When do opposites attract? When they are opposite in sex and sex-role attitudes. *Journal of Personality and Social Psychology* 25:15-20.

Spence, J. T., Helmreich, R., and Stapp, J. 1975. Ratings of self and peers on sex role attributes and their relation to self-esteem and conceptions of masculinity and femininity. *Journal of Personality and Social Psychology* 32:29-39.

Spensley, J., and Barter, J. T. 1971. The adolescent transvestite on a psychiatric service: Family patterns. *Archives of Sexual Behavior* 1:347-56.

Stoller, R. J. 1972. Etiological factors in female transsexualism: A first approximation. *Archives of Sexual Behavior* 2:47-64.

Swenson, C. H. 1955. Sexual differentiation on the Draw-a-Person Test. *Journal of Clinical Psychology* 11:37-41.

Terman, L., and Miles, C. C. 1936. *Sex and personality: Studies in masculinity and femininity.* New York: McGraw-Hill.

Thompson, N. L., and McCandless, B. R. 1976. The homosexual orientation and its antecedents. In *Child Personality and Psychopathology: Current Topics*, ed. A. Davis, 3:in press. New York: Wiley Interscience.

Wolowitz, H. M. 1971. The validity of the psychoanalytic theory of paranoid dynamics. *Psychiatry* 34:358-77.

Index

7 de 3 15
18